Die erste Walpurgisnacht

RECENT RESEARCHES IN MUSIC

A-R Editions publishes seven series of critical editions, spanning the history of Western music, American music, and oral traditions.

RECENT RESEARCHES IN THE MUSIC OF THE MIDDLE AGES AND EARLY RENAISSANCE
Charles M. Atkinson, general editor

RECENT RESEARCHES IN THE MUSIC OF THE RENAISSANCE
James Haar, general editor

RECENT RESEARCHES IN THE MUSIC OF THE BAROQUE ERA
Christoph Wolff, general editor

RECENT RESEARCHES IN THE MUSIC OF THE CLASSICAL ERA
Neal Zaslaw, general editor

RECENT RESEARCHES IN THE MUSIC OF THE NINETEENTH AND EARLY TWENTIETH CENTURIES
Rufus Hallmark, general editor

RECENT RESEARCHES IN AMERICAN MUSIC
John M. Graziano, general editor

RECENT RESEARCHES IN THE ORAL TRADITIONS OF MUSIC
Philip V. Bohlman, general editor

Each edition in *Recent Researches* is devoted to works by a single composer or to a single genre. The content is chosen for its high quality and historical importance and is edited according to the scholarly standards that govern the making of all reliable editions.

For information on establishing a standing order to any of our series, or for editorial guidelines on submitting proposals, please contact:

A-R Editions, Inc.
Middleton, Wisconsin

800 736-0070 (North American book orders)
608 836-9000 (phone)
608 831-8200 (fax)
http://www.areditions.com

ENT RESEARCHES IN THE MUSIC OF THE NINETEENTH AND EARLY TWENTIETH CENTURIES, 49

Felix Mendelssohn Bartholdy

Die erste Walpurgisnacht

First Complete Version, 1832–33

Edited by John Michael Cooper

A-R Editions, Inc.
Middleton, Wisconsin

To Douglass Seaton: satus, philologus, illuminatio

Performance parts are available from the publisher.

A-R Editions, Inc., Middleton, Wisconsin

Printed in the United States of America

ISBN-13: 978-0-89579-624-0
ISBN-10: 0-89579-624-4
ISSN: 0193-5364

♾ The paper used in this publication meets the minimum requirements of the American National Standard for Information Sciences—Permanence of Paper for Printed Library Materials, ANSI Z39.48-1992.

Contents

Acknowledgments ix

Introduction xi

The Historical and Poetic Subject xi
Chronology: Composition, Performance, and Publication of Mendelssohn's *Walpurgisnacht* Settings xiii
Mendelssohn's Musical Interpretation of Goethe's Poem xvii
The Differences between the 1833 and 1844 Versions xxi
A Word on the Appendices xxiii
Notes xxiv

Notes on Performance xxvii

Tempo xxvii
Roles and Casting xxvii
Ensemble Issues xxviii
Performances in English xxix
Notes xxx

Text and Translation xxxi

Plates xxxv

Die erste Walpurgisnacht

No. 1: Einleitung

Overture: Das schlechte Wetter 3
Bad Weather
Der Übergang zum Frühling 63
The Transition to Spring

Strophe 1: "Es lacht der Mai!" (Druide 1) 73
"Now May again" (Druid 1)

Strophe 2: "Die Flamme lodre durch den Rauch!" (Druide 1 und Chor der Druiden) 80
"In sacrifice the flame shall rise" (Druid 1 and Chorus of Druids)

Strophe 3: "Könnt ihr so verwegen handeln?" (Alte Frau) 96
"Know ye not a deed so daring?" (Old Woman)

Strophe 4: "Auf des Lagers hohem Walle" (Alte Frau und Chor der Weiber) 100
"On their ramparts they will slaughter" (Old Woman and Chorus of Women)

Strophe 5: "Wer Opfer heut' zu bringen scheut" (Druide 1) 103
"The man who flies our sacrifice" (Druid 1)

Strophe 6: "Verteilt euch, wackre Männer, hier" (Chor der Wächter des Heidenvolks) 114
"Disperse, disperse, ye gallant men" (Chorus of Guards of the Pagan People)

No. 2

Strophe 7: "Diese dumpfen Pfaffenchristen" (Druide 1) 127
"Should our Christian foes assail us" (Druid 1)

"Kommt mit Zacken und mit Gabeln" (Chor der Wächter des Heidenvolks) 129
"Come! with flappers, Fire and clappers" (Chorus of Guards of the Pagan People)

Strophe 8: "Kommt mit Zacken und mit Gabeln" (Chor des Heidenvolks) 144
"Come with flappers, Fire and clappers" (Chorus of Pagan People)

Strophe 9: "So weit gebracht" (Druide 2 und Chor der Druiden) 194
"Restrain'd by might" (Druid 2 and Chorus of Druids)

Strophe 10: "Hilf, ach hilf mir, Kriegsgeselle!" (Christlicher Wächter) 208
"Help, my Comrades, see a Legion" (Christian Guard)

Strophe 11: "Schreckliche, verhexte Leiber" (Christlicher Wächter und Chor der christlichen Wächter) 213
"See the horrid Haggards gliding" (Christian Guard and Chorus of Christian Guards)

Strophe 12: "Die Flamme reinigt sich vom Rauch" (Druide 2 und Chor der Druiden und des Heidenvolks) 226
"Unclouded now, the flame is bright!" (Druid 2 and Chorus of Druids and Pagan People)

Appendix I: Passages from No. 1 Excised or Revised after ca. July 1831

1. Between mm. 48 and 49 244
2. Between mm. 64 and 65 246
3. Between mm. 82 and 83 248
4. Between mm. 201 and 202 250
5. Original reading of mm. 225–30 252
6. Between mm. 247 and 248 254
7. Between mm. 507 and 508 256
8. Between mm. 689 and 690 260
9. Between mm. 702 and 703 261
10. Between mm. 723 and 724 262

Appendix II: Passages from No. 2 Excised or Revised after ca. July 1831

1. Instead of mm. 1–20 267
2. Between mm. 54 and 55 269
3. Between mm. 149 and 150 270
4. Original readings of mm. 283–84 272
5. Original reading of mm. 317–23 278
6. Between mm. 364 and 365 281
7. Original reading of mm. 394–98 282
8. Original reading of mm. 451–69 285
9. Original reading of mm. 512–16 288
10. Original reading of mm. 534–54 290
11. Between mm. 568 and 569 293

Appendix III: Mendelssohn's Piano-Duet Arrangement of the Overture 297

Critical Report

Sources 317
Editorial Methods 319
Critical Notes 321
1. Text-Genetic Remarks 321
2. Notational Variants 324
3. Other Textual Variants 325
4. Notes on the Appendices 326
Notes 327

Acknowledgments

Thanks are due to the following institutions for permitting the use of their resources in preparing this edition: the Biblioteka Jagiellońska, Kraków (Zdzisław Pietzyk); the Bibliothèque nationale de France (Catherine Massip); the Bodleian Library, Oxford (Peter Ward Jones); the British Library (Nicolas Bell); the J. Pierpont Morgan Library, New York (J. Rigbie Turner); the Museum of Educational Heritage, Tamagawa University, Tokyo (Imai Yoshiko); the Staatsbibliothek zu Berlin–Preußischer Kulturbesitz (Hellmut Hell and Roland Schmidt-Hensel); and the Yushodo Press, Tokyo (Naoko Ideno). For vital support in the final stages of research and production I owe a deep debt of gratitude to Southwestern University, Georgetown, Texas; and for generous support in funding preparatory research for the edition I thank the University of North Texas, Denton, Texas.

For personal assistance and private communications on any number of minor and major matters related to the edition, I am especially grateful to Jonathan Bellman, Clive Brown, Malcolm Gillies, Christoph Hellmundt, Christopher Hogwood, Hiromi Hoshino, Jeffrey Kallberg, Hans-Günter Klein, Kristin Krahe, Julie D. Prandi, Nancy B. Reich, John Rink, Christian Martin Schmidt, Douglass Seaton, Jeffrey S. Sposato, R. Larry Todd, Ralf Wehner, Marian Wilson Kimber, and Pietro Zappalà. Much gratitude is owed also to Dave Lindsey, Morris Martin, Mark McKnight, and Lynne Wright, all of the Willis Library at the University of North Texas, for their assistance in all manner of bibliographic and technical issues in the research and other preparations. Finally, I wish to thank David Utterback at Southwestern University for his valuable assistance in preparing (and repairing) the piano part for the piano-vocal score.

Most of all, as ever, I wish to thank Cindy for her patience, assistance, and encouragement at every turn along the way.

Introduction

The composition to which the present volume is devoted represents an extraordinary instance in the annals of nineteenth-century history. It is a work by a composer of international stature that is based on a text by a close friend and personal mentor who was also a great poet and cultural luminary. Its subject is not only potently invested with historical fact and religious belief, but also remarkably relevant to the issues of conflict and tolerance, identity and alterity that remain central to twentieth- and twenty-first-century social and artistic discourse. Its devoutly Lutheran composer of Jewish heritage was and is celebrated for his contributions to sacred music—predominantly Christian sacred music—but in this work he adopts a musical stance that at some level celebrates not Christianity, but its pagan foes. Its music represents a milestone in the nineteenth century's exploration of large-scale cyclical unity and thematic and motivic transformation. Finally, it is the first complete version of a work that the composer overhauled and published more than a decade later, standing at a substantially different position in his own career as a public figure engaged with the text's profoundly symbolic social and religious themes. The similarities and differences between the two versions' interpretation of their shared poetic text thus offer complementary insights into developments in the composer's style and musical persona over the course of that decade.

The work in question, of course, is the early version of *Die erste Walpurgisnacht* (The First Walpurgis Night), composed by Felix Mendelssohn Bartholdy (1809–47) in 1830–33 on a text by Johann Wolfgang von Goethe (1749–1832). In its final version, published in 1844 as opus 60, the *Walpurgisnacht* ranked among Mendelssohn's most popular works through the first decade of the twentieth century. It quickly garnered attention as a musical masterpiece, a significant cultural statement submitted by one of Europe's most sought-after conductors, composers, and educators.

But the final version of the *Walpurgisnacht* differs substantially from Mendelssohn's original conception of Goethe's ballad. The composer's correspondence reveals that he considered arranging for at least one subsequent performance of the early version and even for publishing it, but events forestalled these plans. By the time he had any realistic hope of being able to pursue them, the version of 1832–33 was already something of an "old piece."[1] When he returned to the project in the early 1840s his penchant for revision led him to rework it far more extensively than he had earlier envisioned—and so the revised version eclipsed its predecessor, in the event obscuring a remarkable composition that documented a public musical career that had already scored significant triumphs.[2]

Several considerations justify a modern revival of the early version of Mendelssohn's *Walpurgisnacht* cantata—without either disparaging the final version or relegating the early one to the status of a curiosity. First, the early version's music, interpretation of Goethe's text, and quasi-dramatic depiction of Goethe's scenic treatment of his subject are sufficiently different from the familiar version to qualify this version as an almost entirely autonomous work. Second, although Mendelssohn evidently found that this original setting of Goethe's text was no longer representative of his approach to the poem in the early 1840s, it nevertheless offers a compelling view of his artistic and personal reception of the text and its subject during the early years of his artistic maturity. Finally, the artistic accomplishment Mendelssohn had attained by the early 1830s is attested to not least of all by its compositional context: it is coeval with the final versions of the *Midsummer Night's Dream* and *Hebrides* Overtures as well as his concentrated work on the "Italian" and "Reformation" Symphonies and the beginnings of work on the landmark oratorio *St. Paul.*

The Historical and Poetic Subject

For nineteenth-century Europeans the subject of Goethe's ballad represented an epic clash of ideologies and faiths that reached back more than a millennium into European history and culminated in the eighth century during the reign of the Frankish king Charlemagne (Charles the Great, fl. 768–814). In the eighth century Western Christendom was geographically divided and interspersed among non-Christian peoples who were often hostile toward them and their beliefs: in addition to the Umayyad Empire (representing the comparatively new religion of Islam), whose military expansion before the Battle of Tours in 732 carried it into Spain and the Frankish lands themselves, the lands between the Rhine and Elbe rivers were the province of the pagan Saxon tribes, historically known as some of Europe's fiercest warriors. This inherently unstable situation resulted in a strong theocratic alliance between the Roman church and the Frankish kings, aimed at protecting Christendom's constituents from hostility and, of course, spreading the religion itself. But the alliance was unable to prevent outbreaks of violence within pagan and Christian territories alike. After Charles assumed the throne in 768 he resolved that the only way to deal with the pagans was "to attack the treacherous and treaty-breaking tribe of the Saxons and to persist in this war until they were either defeated and forced to accept the Christian religion or entirely exterminated"[3]—a decision that led to the three decades of bloody military campaigns now generally known as the Saxon Wars.

Seemingly unique in this chronicle of territorial and religious conflicts is the figure after whom the Walpurgis Night was named: St. Walpurgis (Walburg/Walburga/Walpurga; ca. 710–79), an Anglo-Saxon missionary nun. Walpurgis traveled to the Continent in 748 in response to the appeal of her uncle, St. Boniface, newly designated archbishop of Mainz and primate of Germany, for the British Isles' women to aid in the administering of Christianity to the pagan populace. Unlike many other major characters in the century's chronicle of religious turbulence, however, Walpurgis cultivated beneficence and charity and remained distant from any associations with violence, healing the ailments of her pagan subjects while also evangelizing as abbess of the double monastery (home to both men and women clerics) at Heidenheim, Franconia, from 760 until her death. Her reputation as a healer accounts for her role as patron saint against a variety of misfortunes ranging from plague, famine, coughs, and rabies, to dog bites and storms. In addition, thanks to her outstanding education she was able to write a biography of St. Winibald (her brother) and an account in Latin of St. Willibald's travels in Palestine; because of these contributions she is also distinguished as one of the Christian church's earliest women authors in England and Germany. She died on 25 April 779 and was canonized in 870.

In the Roman martyrology Walpurgis is celebrated on 1 May—a date also associated with Beltane, the celebration of springtime and fertility cultivated by the pagans whose traditions she strove to overturn through benevolence rather than force. The date thus represented a paradoxical convergence of paganism and Christianity, of the ancient and the (comparably) new. Writings by authors ranging from Christian August Vulpius (eventual brother-in-law to Goethe), the Austrian novelist Karoline Pichler, and the Swiss writer Heinrich Zschokke, to major figures such as Theodor Storm, Bram Stoker, Karl Kraus, Thomas Mann, Ogden Nash, and Edward Albee have explored in prose the same formidable conflict between reason and faith, natural and supernatural, good and evil that occasioned not only Goethe's ballad and Mendelssohn's cantata, but also the "Walpurgisnacht" scene in the first part of the great poet's recounting of the Faust legend and the "Klassische Walpurgisnacht" in the tragedy's second part. Indeed, apart from the Faust legend itself, few literary topoi were as familiar to nineteenth-century Europeans through a variety of artistic approaches as was the subject of the Walpurgis Night.

In addition, in the mid- and late eighteenth century enlightened thinkers began to seek a logical historical explanation for the legends and lore surrounding the Walpurgis Night. Typical of these conjectures is the explanation offered by Friedrich Maurer in 1796. Postulating that the Saxons "valued their fathers' religion no less than their freedom [from foreign dominion]," Maurer proposed that they

> turned to guile so that they would be able to participate in their sacrificial ceremonies. They wrapped themselves in horrifying disguises and cleared the path to their idols at night by scaring the sentinels, who took flight all the more quickly at the sight of these devilish forms because those who were taking part in the evening procession [up the mountain] were ready for anything, armed with pitchforks and torches.
>
> The Christians of that time considered idolatry devil-worship, and they were absolutely convinced that despite the Christian sentinels who were guarding the paths to the sacrificial places, the devil himself was supporting his disciples and carrying them through the air.[4]

Written in 1799, Goethe's ballad "Die erste Walpurgisnacht" mediates between the night's fantastic lore of witchcraft and demons and the equally imaginative approach adopted by Maurer and others of his ilk. The theme of the historical clash between paganism and Christianity is central to the poem. After establishing this conflict-ridden historical context and portraying the Christian missionaries as armed zealots who murder the pagans' women and children (strophes 1–6), it recounts a Saxon ruse to scare away the Christians by carrying out a masquerade of a witches' sabbath on the Harz Mountains' highest peak, the Brocken (strophes 7 and 8). The trick succeeds, and the "dumpfen Pfaffenchristen" (foolish cleric-Christians) abandon their posts, convinced that the devil and his hordes are upon them (strophes 10 and 11). The Christian guards' strophes are interfolded into two strophes depicting the pagans themselves as they celebrate their rites atop the mountain—but the universalist message of their ceremonies, celebrating the *Allvater* (literally, "all-father") for the light he sheds on humanity, centers on the classic eighteenth- and nineteenth-century metaphor for intellectual enlightenment and spiritual edification. If the poem's historical sympathies lie more with the pagans than with their Christian adversaries, its spiritual and religious ones are equally consistent with the values and mores of enlightened late-eighteenth-century Christian society.

Because the subject of Goethe's ballad would have been familiar to many of his readers, performers and audiences who encountered the text in Mendelssohn's setting would have had some appreciation of its historical, religious, and societal substance. Nevertheless, the poem's paradoxical and (for Goethe) characteristically irreverent sympathies would have complicated the task of appreciating its message. In order to provide some rudimentary interpretive guidelines for contemporary listeners, at least two early performances of Mendelssohn's setting included the following brief explanatory note in the concert program, where it appears in parentheses and quotation marks, although the source is not identified:

> During the last years of paganism in Germany, the Christians declared that the druids' sacrifices were punishable by death. Nevertheless, at the beginning of springtime the druids and the populace sought to regain the peaks of the mountains, make their sacrifices there, and intimidate and scare off the Christian warriors (usually through the latter's fear of the devil). The legend of the first Walpurgis Night is supposed to be based on these attempts.[5]

When Mendelssohn published his cantata, the printed German and English first editions replaced this historical explanation with another, more symbolic one, which Goethe sent to the composer when he learned of his plans to set the ballad to music.[6] Coupled with the insights offered by Mendelssohn's plentiful remarks concerning his work on the piece, these two explanations offer useful guidelines for understanding Goethe's poem and Mendelssohn's interpretation of it.

Chronology: Composition, Performance, and Publication of Mendelssohn's *Walpurgisnacht* Settings

Precisely when Mendelssohn began planning his setting of Goethe's Walpurgis Night poem is unclear. In a way the poem was directed toward Mendelssohn from the outset, for Goethe wrote it on 30 July 1799 and sent it to Mendelssohn's future composition teacher, Karl Friedrich Zelter (1758–1832), less than a month later. Zelter reportedly tried to set the ballad on three separate occasions (in 1799, 1802, and 1812)—but in vain. Prior to the last attempt he asked the great poet for some explanatory information to aid him in his task.[7] Goethe responded at length:

> But I still have to respond to your inquiry regarding "Die erste Walpurgisnacht." The answer goes something like this. Among historians there are some—and they are men to whom one cannot deny respect who seek a real basis for every fable and every tradition, no matter how absurd, and who always believe that they have found a factual core in the wrappings of every fairy tale.
>
> We owe a great deal of good to this approach, for to make prose out of such poetry requires a great deal of knowledge or indeed spirit, cleverness, and imagination, just for starters. So it is that one of the investigators of German antiquity has wished to discover a historical origin for the witches' and devils' ride on the Brocken, which has been known in Germany since time immemorial, in order to rescue and justify it. Thus, the German pagan priests and elders, after they had been driven out of their sacred groves and Christianity had been forced on the populace, withdrew with their faithful followers into the desolate, inaccessible Harz mountains in the early spring, so that they could offer up their prayers and their fires to the incorporeal god of heaven and earth, according to ancient custom. To protect themselves from the spying, armed converts [to Christianity] they decided that it was advisable to disguise some of their members and thereby to keep their superstitious adversaries at a distance, and thus protected by devils' masks to carry out the purest of worship services.
>
> I happened upon this explanation somewhere or other many years ago; I couldn't tell you who the author was. The idea appealed to me, and so I have made this marvelous history back into a poetic fable.[8]

Zelter never was able to rise to the challenge of Goethe's "poetic fable." The idea was planted in fertile soil, however, for when he formally introduced the twelve-year-old prodigy to the poet nearly six decades his senior in 1821 he initiated one of the most remarkable intergenerational artistic relationships in the annals of Western history. It is tempting to imagine that Zelter informed Mendelssohn of how his relationship with Goethe had begun and that this history then led the precocious youth to undertake the challenge his own teacher had declined.

A little-known letter from Mendelssohn to his friend Franz Hauser reveals that the composer had developed ideas for at least strophes 9 and/or 12 by the fall of 1830,[9] but the notion of setting the text probably originated even earlier, in discussions with members of his family or other immediate circles that were not recorded in writing. In any case, it was already a "favorite old scheme" by the time Mendelssohn commenced work on the project in February 1831. Inspired by Fanny Hensel's revival of the family's Sunday musicales *(Sonntagsmusiken)*, he reported its inception in a letter to Hensel dated 22 February 1831:

> I cannot tell you how greatly the new Sunday musicales please me. That is a brilliant idea, and I beg you for God's sake not to let it fall by the wayside again, but rather to commission your traveling brother to write something new for you. He will do it gladly, for he is all too delighted with you and your idea.... One of my pieces probably already owes its birth to these Sunday musicales. When you wrote to me about [the idea] recently I wondered whether I might not be able to send you something for them, and then a favorite old scheme of mine occurred to me again—but it became so extended that I cannot [yet] give it to Emil[10] to bring along, so he will have to bring it later. Listen and marvel[!] Since leaving Vienna I have halfway composed Goethe's "Die erste Walpurgisnacht," but do not yet have the courage to write it out. The thing has now taken shape but has become a grand cantata with full orchestra. It can become very merry, for at the beginning it is full of spring songs and more such things; and then, when the guards make a ruckus with their prongs and pitchforks and owls, there is also the witches' spookiness, and [you] know that I have a particular fondness for that. Then the druids who make the sacrifices appear in C major with their trombones, and then again the guards, who are afraid of them (here I mean to introduce an eerie, lightly mysterious chorus); and then finally, at the end, the complete sacrificial hymn. Don't you think that this could become a new kind of cantata? As a matter of course there is an instrumental introduction, and the whole thing is lively enough. I think it will be finished soon.[11]

Just over a week later, on 5 March, Mendelssohn informed Goethe of his scheme:

> I also have time during the penitential season to compose in peace and diligently. What has occupied me almost exclusively for several weeks is my music to the poem titled "Die erste Walpurgisnacht" by Your Excellency. I want to compose it as a kind of grand cantata with orchestra, and the

merry beginning of spring, then the witchery and devilish magic, and the solemn sacrificial chorus throughout, could provide the opportunity for the most beautiful music. I do not know whether I will succeed in it, but I sense how large the task is and how collectedly and honorably I must undertake it.[12]

By 29 March he still had no ideas for the overture, but he remained hopeful that once he had accomplished that, "the thing will have come together and I will write it out in a couple of days."[13] The prediction of rapid progress turned out to be premature, however, for a letter to his family from Naples reports that he was preoccupied with the *Walpurgisnacht* and had "to get back to [his] witches":

This entire letter is actually cloaked in uncertainty—or rather, I am cloaked in uncertainty as to whether I should use the bass drum. "Prongs, pitchforks, and rattling sticks" actually do make me inclined to use it, but moderation disinclines me. I am certainly the only one ever to have composed the Blocksberg[14] without using piccolo, but I would be sorry to forgo the bass drum. I'm afraid that the *Walpurgisnacht* will be finished and packed up, and that I'll be traveling the countryside again and writing about God knows what, before Fanny's advice reaches me. I'm convinced that Fanny would say to use it, but I'm still undecided. A great deal of noise must be made in any case.[15]

The work's completion continued to elude him. He reported from Naples on 10 May that it was "not yet finished ... because it [was] growing rapidly,"[16] and in an undated letter that probably stems from the summer of 1831 he ascribes its composition to Rome—also referring to the work as "a grand symphony with chorus, or rather a chorus with collaborative symphony."[17] On 13 July, then, he finally was able to issue another confident report on the composition, addressed to the baritone Eduard Devrient:

In the meantime I have also written another large composition that may also be able to have some broader effect: *Die erste Walpurgisnacht* by Goethe. I started on it just because I liked it and it spoke to me; [at the time] I wasn't considering it for performance. But now that it sits completed before me I see that it would work very well as a grand concert composition. In my first subscription concert in Berlin you will have to sing [the role of] the bearded druid-priest; the choruses will be performed by [X] with the generous participation of [Y] etc., etc. I wrote the part of the priest so that it lies well in your throat, with your permission; so you'll once again have to project it. Just as it has so far been my experience that those works that I have written with the least consideration of the public have always pleased the public best, I believe it will it be that way in this instance too. I write this just so that you'll see that I'm thinking of *practical* matters—albeit only after the fact. But any devil who presumes to compose music, which is the most unpractical thing in the world (this is precisely why I love it), and in so doing think about practical matters, might as well set his thoughts of love for his beloved into rhymes and verses and present them to her in that form.[18]

On 14 July 1831 he reported to his family that he had worked out the conclusion of the cantata and that the following day the whole would be truly finished—except for the overture, which might take the form of either an extended symphony or "eine kurze Frühlingseinleitung" (a short springtime introduction). He also reported that he had improved the ending:

Now the ending has become better than even I imagined it would. The monsters and the bearded druid with his trombones that stand blasting away behind him made some royal fun for me; I spent a couple of mornings very happily with that.[19]

Although the cantata evidently still lacked its overture, Mendelssohn was sufficiently confident in his new composition to inscribe the date on the final page of the score on the following day (source *AS1*; see plate 2); his diary entry for 17 July 1831 records that it had been further "geputzt" (tidied up) by then.[20] By 24 July he had played it for Carl Mozart, who was so impressed that he suggested that it should be published right away.[21] The composer, however, insisted on trying out the new work in one of the Mendelssohn family's Sunday musicales first. From Lucerne he wrote to Devrient:

I wish that I could *really* be with you some evening and play my *Walpurgisnacht* for you—or rather, that you could sing it for me; it lies very well for your voice. But write to me whether you can hit the high F—not sustained, but just for a quarter note. It occurs near the end.[22]

The following two weeks produced the most substantive information to date on the content of the work as it existed at that point: an exchange of letters between Mendelssohn and Goethe. On 28 August Mendelssohn wrote:

I wrote to you already from Rome that I had the audacity to compose your "Erste Walpurgisnacht." I have in the meantime finished it, while in Milan. It turned out as a kind of cantata for chorus and orchestra, longer and more distended than I initially envisioned, because the longer I carried it around with me the more extended, grand, and appealing the task became. Permit me to express my gratitude for the heavenly text. When the old druid brings his sacrifice and the whole thing becomes solemn and incomparably grand, there is no need to write music—it is already so clearly present and everything already resonates so greatly that I always sang the verses to myself without meaning to. If I can find a good chorus and an opportunity in Munich, whither I depart tomorrow, I will try to perform it there. My only hope is that people will hear in my music how deeply I have felt the beauty of the text.[23]

The elder poet responded with an explanation of the poem's symbolic implications:

It pleases me greatly that you have dedicated yourself so seriously to "Die erste Walpurgisnacht," for no one has been able to make anything out of this poem, not even our excellent Zelter. It is intended as elevated symbolism[24] in the literal sense. For in the history of the world it must eternally be repeated that something old, established, proven, [and] reassuring will be compacted, pushed aside, dislocated, and, if not abolished, then corralled into the tightest space by emergent new forces. The middle period, in which the hatred is still capable of reacting, and still may do so, is presented here succinctly enough, and a joyous, indestructible enthusiasm flares up once again with brilliance and clarity. I'm certain you have brought life and significance to all this. May it therefore likewise thrive in my [own] joyous pleasure.[25]

As of fall 1831, then, the *Walpurgisnacht* was sufficiently complete in Mendelssohn's view for him to write to Goethe about it and about his hopes of arranging for a performance. But a significant obstacle remained—for he still had little or nothing in the way of an overture. He was finally able to report progress on "the Saxon A-minor overture that [was] to precede the *Walpurgisnacht*" when he wrote to Fanny from Paris on 21 January 1832, and he finished the initial version of the overture on 4 February.[26] After another pass through for revisions, he inscribed the final page of the score once again on 13 February (see plate 2). That same day, writing from Paris, he reported on the work to his family:

> My A-minor overture is finished; it represents bad weather. A couple of days ago I finished an introduction representing the thaw and the arrival of springtime, then numbered the pages of the *Walpurgisnacht* [i.e., the texted part of the cantata], tidied up the seven movements a little, and confidently wrote "Paris, in February" beneath "Milan, in July." I think you all will like it.[27]

Goethe never heard Mendelssohn's setting of his "poetic fable," for he died on 22 March 1832. The loss cast a long shadow over Mendelssohn's emotional well-being for months to come, and his physical well-being was compromised when he contracted cholera during the great scourge that swept Paris that spring. In mid-April he was finally able to leave for London—home to some of his more significant musical triumphs of 1829 and the final main station in his grand tour. There, on 30 April, he performed his newly completed setting of the late poet's "Walpurgisnacht" for his close friends Ignaz and Charlotte Moscheles—a performance that may account for the piano-duet arrangement of the overture (source *APf1*; see plate 3).[28]

But two weeks later death struck again, this time claiming the life of Zelter. This deep personal and professional loss put the young composer in a difficult position. He had spent two full years broadening his horizons, establishing strong personal and professional relationships with most of musical Europe, and preparing for a career as an independent professional musician. He was now the toast of London's musical society. But he also found himself strongly pressured to apply for the position of Zelter's successor as director of the Berlin Singakademie—a position he had little realistic hope of attaining, and one that (if attained) would leave him vulnerable to suspicions of having benefited from his family's means and influence. Mendelssohn was fully aware that the stolid disposition of the Singakademie would almost inevitably favor his less brilliant but far more established competitors, but once he had decided to apply for the post he pursued his candidacy with characteristic energy.[29] Chief among the ventures intended to remind the Berliners of his talent and breadth as composer and conductor were three concerts given over the course of the winter for the benefit of the widows of the Royal Orchestra. These concerts provided the occasion, finally, for the public premiere of *Die erste Walpurgisnacht*.[30]

After more than eighteen months of circulating the cantata only in private circles, Mendelssohn now moved decisively to present it to the public. A performance on 11 October 1832 in one of Fanny Hensel's Sunday musicales not only realized his earlier wish to have the work performed in that venue[31] and offered his family and friends a chance to hear the work about which they had already heard much, but also gave him a chance to make practical changes and test its suitability for public performance. The *Walpurgisnacht* was afforded pride of place in the concert of 10 January 1833, serving as the *de facto* finale to the series and suggesting that Mendelssohn viewed it as a summative finale to his compositional career up to that point. The gesture did not go unnoticed: the influential critic Ludwig Rellstab, for one, proposed in a review of the public premiere (and of the series of three concerts to which it belonged), that "These three musical evenings were more meaningful for the art than a whole year of the usual concerts."[32]

Although Mendelssohn's benefit concerts were well attended and well received, the reviewers also suggested that the music's merits did not wholly obscure the signs of the composer's youth. Rellstab, who had expressed his wish with regard to the first concert (and the "Reformation" Symphony in particular) that "the composer would adhere less to colossal things than to beautiful essentials,"[33] discussed the *Walpurgisnacht* in some detail in a review of the concert of 10 January:

> The second half of the concert comprised a longer musical composition by Herr Mendelssohn for voices and orchestra. The composer's subject was provided by Goethe's poem "Die erste Walpurgisnacht," which explains the historical circumstances behind the magic festival at the peak of the Blocksberg and thus (or perhaps nevertheless) is romantic. In a grand instrumental introduction, which to us seemed too long, the composer offers an image of the whole. In this section the composer was inspired by essentially the same challenges that Spohr had to address in his *Faust* and (after him) Weber in his *Freischütz*.[34] We would have some objections to the treatment of the text (although this would involve too much detail for these pages), but the work is equally rich in individual beauties, fantastic moments, and bold combinations; the choruses are particularly effective. So disruptive were the overly crowded hall (in the lower level there was hardly even standing room left), the considerable heat, and the early departure of some listeners that this reviewer, too, left early (after the original and fantastic chorus "Kommt mit Zacken, kommt mit Gabeln") in order to reserve for himself the freer enjoyment of the conclusion at some future occasion. He therefore does not permit himself to judge the whole. He did, however, get the impression that up to that point the work dispensed with the cantilena that is so necessary for the voice, and for which the poem provides not a few opportunities.[35]

A correspondent for the Leipzig *Allgemeine Musikalische Zeitung* was similarly impressed, if also more frank in voicing his conservative objections:

> The second part of the concert was filled by a new cantata by Felix Mendelssohn-Bartholdy: "Die erste Walpurgisnacht," a

poem by Goethe that is more fantastic than lyrical. In this composition, with its almost excessive orchestral outlay, we see the composer rich in musical invention for instrumental works, often in ways approaching Beethoven's last works. This was evident already in the very long introduction. Some vocal solos for the tenor (Herr Mantius) were original and melodious, and the choruses were for the most part appropriate to the subject—unearthly, bizarre, and vigorous. But on the whole this grand vocal piece, excellently performed by the large orchestral forces of the Royal Kapelle, was not as generally gripping as expected. This probably is attributable to the lack of pronounced melody, the poem itself, and the too obvious reliance [of the music] on modulations and instrumental effects. This third concert was exceedingly well attended.[36]

The concerts—especially the one that included the *Walpurgisnacht*—made a lasting impact on members of Mendelssohn's immediate circles. His mother, Lea, implicitly praised the cantata (along with his other original works performed in the series) when she sized up developments in the ongoing contest for the Singakademie directorship in a letter to the violinist Ferdinand David shortly after the premiere:

> Felix's three benefit concerts for the fund of the widows of the orchestra are now over, and they aroused much enthusiasm and interest. If he and his compositions are too original for *le gros de public*,[37] they nevertheless arouse true enthusiasm among those whose tastes concur with his own; through them he has won a multitude of fans.[38]

Even more impressed was Fanny Hensel, who came to know the work—evidently by singing the part of the old pagan woman in strophe 3 (mm. 586–667) of Part I[39]—during her time with Felix in the summer of 1832. Writing in May 1833, Hensel described the cantata as "one of the most interesting pieces of music that there is."[40] She also confided to her diary that Lea Mendelssohn had been singing part of the "Kommt mit Zacken" chorus (mm. 90–388 in Part II) sometime in mid-May 1833. With tongue-in-cheek humor, Fanny reports that her son, Sebastian (then nearly three years old), heard his grandmother's tune and asked who had written it—whereupon Lea answered that it was by Goethe, who had written "many songs."[41]

Hensel retained her enthusiasm about the *Walpurgisnacht* long after the Berlin premiere. She wrote enthusiastically about the cantata in late February 1834, asking the composer whether and when he planned to perform it in Düsseldorf (where he was Municipal Music Director) and requesting that he send her the score for a few weeks.[42] She repeated the request shortly after he had taken up his new position as kapellmeister of the famed Gewandhaus Orchestra in Leipzig, and referred to it again (in an allusion to the finale of Beethoven's Ninth Symphony) early in 1836.[43] Although there seems to be no surviving documentation of when Fanny came into possession of the manuscript for the early version, she clearly did so—for her penciled handwriting is present on several pages, including some containing deleted material (see plate 4).

And what of Mendelssohn's own use of the early version after the public premiere? In April 1834 he was still planning to perform it in Düsseldorf and then to publish it. In response to Hensel's February 1834 request that he send her the score, he wrote on 7 April that he hoped to perform it in a concert of 4 May ("hopefully in fair weather").[44] Ultimately, however, his characteristic self-doubts got the better of him. He did not conduct the 1832–33 version of the *Walpurgisnacht* in any documented concerts from his Düsseldorf years,[45] and although the envisioned improvements were evidently still sufficiently limited that they could be worked out in the score and then transferred to the original parts in the event of a Leipzig performance when he moved to Leipzig in August 1835, no further performances of the version of 1832–33 ever occurred. The surviving evidence permits secure conjecture on several points concerning the status of the *Walpurgisnacht* cantata at that point in Mendelssohn's career. As late as 1837 he was still sufficiently convinced with his earlier setting to discuss it with Schumann,[46] and he still thought of the work as comprising two large parts rather than the nine shorter movements of the final version. At least the bulk of his reservations concerned Part I (strophes 1–6 of Goethe's poem).

In any event, *Die erste Walpurgisnacht* disappears from Mendelssohn's correspondence until the symphonic breakthrough of the early 1840s that resulted in the performance and publication of the symphony-cantata *Lobgesang*, op. 52, and the Symphony no. 3 in A Minor, op. 56 ("Scottish"). A letter of 18 November 1840 to his friend Klingemann in London reveals that by that point he had come to think of it as a genre-counterpart to the *Lobgesang*,[47] but the project was still languishing in his study when the idea turned up again more than two years later, when he wrote of the plan to his mother that he "would now very much like finally to make the *Walpurgisnacht* into a symphony-cantata. This was my original intention but nothing came of it because I lacked the courage to make it so."[48]

After a hiatus of nearly a decade, the rehabilitation of the *Walpurgisnacht* progressed rapidly. The autograph orchestral score for the revised version bears the date "December 1842,"[49] and by the 11th of that month the revisions were sufficiently complete for Mendelssohn to write of the project in detail, in the past tense, and with conspicuously ironic references to Christian religious traditions:

> On the 21st or 22nd we will give a concert here for the king. In the second half my *Walpurgisnacht* will be resurrected, albeit in a rather different habit than the previous version, which was fed all too generously with trombones and rather scrappily written for the voice. But for this I was obliged to write out the entire score again from A to Z [and] to insert two new movements, to say nothing of the remaining tailoring.[50]

But circumstances—most prominently, the death of Lea Mendelssohn on 12 December 1842—once again conspired against progress on the revision project. By the time he resumed work on it in January 1843, he was able to report to Fanny:

> The business matters and (external) labors are pressing down hard on me once again and making me fairly desolate. On the other hand, writing music in the little room I've set up precisely for that purpose is my best means of consolation and relief. Fortunately, as I've already written to you, I had rewritten the entire *Walpurgisnacht,* but only the four-part choral material because it was to be sung in a week and the rehearsals had already begun. But the whole of the orchestral material still had to be written out, and the multitude of little details that had to be entered were, as I've said, the first and only things that really (not just apparently) occupied me. Now it is finally finished, and I believe that even you, who knew the earlier one so well (better than any soul other than myself), will be amazed at how much better the whole thing is now. I cannot now bear even to think that anyone knows it in its first version; everything that was good in that one and has been retained has only now attained its rightful significance, since the defective and inadequate material has now been deleted and replaced.[51]

Fanny, however, was unconvinced (a response she admitted was typical of her reactions to Felix's revisions):

> I'm also very curious about your revisions of the *Walpurgisnacht.* You know how difficult it is for me to adjust to revisions, but I'll do my best. If only you've retained my lovely alto solo—that gave me great pleasure as a young woman [playing] an old woman. The memory of such triumphs doesn't disappear.[52]

Many essentials of the remainder of the *Walpurgisnacht*'s history are familiar from standard accounts.[53] The revised version was premiered, under Mendelssohn's direction, on 2 February 1843. In its new incarnation the work won the enthusiastic endorsement of Berlioz. The French composer described it in his *Voyage musicale en Allemagne et en Italie* as "a kind of oratorio on Goethe's *Walpurgisnacht*...the finest thing that Mendelssohn has done."[54] He continued:

> One must hear Mendelssohn's music to realize what scope the poem offers a skilful composer. He has made admirable use of his opportunities. The score is of impeccable clarity, notwithstanding the complexity of the writing. Voices and instruments are completely integrated, and interwoven with an apparent confusion which is the perfection of art. I would especially single out, as superb examples of two diametrically opposite genres, the mysterious scene of the posting of the sentinels and the final chorus, in which the voice of the priest rises solemnly and serenely at intervals above the din of the decoy demons and sorcerers. One does not know which to praise most in this finale, the orchestral or the choral writing, or the whirling momentum and sweep of the whole.[55]

Berlioz was not the only one impressed. The critic Oswald Lorenz, writing in the *Neue Zeitschrift für Musik,* called the work "an extraordinarily lovely thing, a cantata—or rather a ballad, as [the composer] would prefer to call it. It has been a long time since I have heard anything so fresh and healthy, anything that brought such joy to one's heart."[56]

Finally, in the summer of 1843 Mendelssohn himself resolved to publish the work. In July–August 1843, after further revisions, he wrote out the first piano-vocal score for the entire work and had a manuscript copy of the orchestral score, to be used for the engraving of the parts and score, produced. The orchestral parts and piano-vocal score were published in February 1844, followed in April by the orchestral score. Thus Mendelssohn's setting of Goethe's ballad finally was "sent out into the world" after a gestation that spanned more than thirteen years.

Mendelssohn's Musical Interpretation of Goethe's Poem

In both incarnations, Mendelssohn's *Walpurgisnacht* cantata represents a remarkable constellation of the issues, ideas, and compositional techniques that were being explored by composers of his generation in the decades following the deaths of Weber, Beethoven, and Schubert. Most obviously noteworthy is its stylistic eclecticism. The "bad weather" overture is a vivid contribution to the tempestuous symphonic style cultivated in Beethoven's middle and late Vienna periods as well as the development and coda of Mendelssohn's *Hebrides* Overture. The second druid entry in the 1832–33 version ("Wer Opfer heut / Zu bringen scheut"; I: mm. 668–743[57]) invokes the rage music of Handelian and contemporary Italian opera. The extended pagan chorus "Kommt mit Zacken" (II: mm. 80–363) exploits a *(faux-)* demonic idiom familiar at the time from Spohr's opera *Faust* and the "Wolf's Glen" scene of Weber's *Der Freischütz* (as Rellstab noted), and most familiar today from the celebrated final movement of Berlioz's *Symphonie fantastique* (the first draft of which Berlioz showed Mendelssohn in Rome in March 1831). The music of the pagans' ceremonial rites in Part II is remarkable not only for the aura of religious exaltation familiar from Beethoven's *Missa solemnis* and Ninth Symphony, but also for its foreshadowing of the inspired style of choral writing that Mendelssohn would bring to further fruition in the *Lobgesang* and the oratorios *St. Paul* (1833–36) and *Elijah* (1846–47). Finally, the history of genre-designations applied to this composition reveals Mendelssohn laboring to break free of traditional generic expectations and identify the *Walpurgisnacht* in terms that would aptly reflect its poetic, narrative, and musical attributes. Initially conceived as "a kind of grand cantata" or "a new kind of cantata," by the summer of 1831 it had become "a grand symphony with chorus, or rather a chorus with collaborative symphony." By 1840–42 the composer had cometo view it as a "symphony-cantata" (i.e., a secular pendant to the *Lobgesang*), while Berlioz referred to it as "a kind of oratorio." Finally, by the time of its publication Mendelssohn had arrived at the designation of "ballad"—i.e., a patently literary genre defined above all by its poetic content and narrative qualities, the importance of which implicitly transcend intrinsically musical characteristics. In a word, these genre-designations reveal the *Walpurgisnacht* as a manifestation of the quandaries that traditional genre-categories posed for many composers of his generation.

Die erste Walpurgisnacht is also a concentrated essay in the nineteenth-century ideology of organicism and the

Example 1.

technique of thematic transformation in multimovement cyclic form. The most important of the cantata's melodic cells is one that generally signifies the theme of the pagans' edification, devotion, and religious rites. References to this cell are recognizable partly by their characteristic pitch contour ($\hat{5}$–$\hat{1}$–$\hat{2}$–$\hat{3}$, ascending), their tendency to begin on an upbeat (often with a repeated note), and their placement at the beginnings of themes, phrases, strophes, or especially important lines of text. The cell remains recognizable also when it is transposed within the triad it outlines and expanded through embellishment of its defining pitches.[58] For a cursory review of some recurrences and transformations of this cell, see example 1.

The other motivic cell—a chromatic descent in the minor mode, usually beginning on $\hat{2}$ or $\hat{6}$—evokes the other salient aspect of the text and historical context of Goethe's ballad: that of strife or conflict. Embedded in the chromatically descending bass line of the main theme in the "bad weather" overture (A–G♯–G♮–F♯–F♮–E; mm. 3–12), this cell allegorically adumbrates the pagan/Christian conflict in the texted portion of the work. It first appears as an autonomous element during one of the more tumultuous passages of the overture (example 2a) and assumes a greater thematic and motivic function when the druid guard first proposes the ruse to scare away the Christians (example 2b). Its prominence increases as more and more of the pagans join in to execute the scheme. By the time of an emphatic tonicization of B-flat (the lowered supertonic) in the "Kommt mit Zacken" chorus (II: mm. 304–21) the charade clearly is well underway; indeed, the direct return by semitone to

Example 2.

(a) I: 279–86

(b) II: 40–45

(c) II: 334–38

(d) II: 502–4

the original tonic (A minor) leads to its most overt statement yet (example 2c), and from this Mendelssohn crafts an extended stretto in Part II, measures 342–64. After a brief but ferocious return during the instrumental interlude that accompanies the change of scene to the druids' rites (II: mm. 389–401), the cell makes one final appearance as the Christian guards collectively tremble at the fearsome devil's-charade they observe before deciding to abandon their posts (example 2d).

But Mendelssohn's efforts to compose his understanding of Goethe's text by no means resulted in a simplistic or dispassionate setting. On the contrary, he also observed several significant abstract poetic principles and realized or reinterpreted them by means of his own elaborations and alterations. The expansions via repetition are perhaps the simplest of these (although they immediately distinguished Mendelssohn's setting of the *Walpurgisnacht* from other contemporary choral ballads). The most prominent example of this technique of elaboration is of course the extended "Kommt mit Zacken" chorus, which occupies 297 of the 571 measures in the "final" version of Part II (i.e., after various cuts but before the 1842–44 revision).

Other alterations are more subtle. In Goethe's poem the male voices clearly predominate: only five of its ninety-nine lines (lines 28–32) are explicitly entrusted to female voices, and another eight (lines 14–17 and 96–99) might implicitly entail female voices as well. Mendelssohn expands the enfranchisement of the female voices: they are not only included in lines 14–17 and 96–99 but also dominate in the extended "Kommt mit Zacken" chorus (lines 60–65). They participate (along with the male chorus—also not indicated in Goethe's poem) in the devotional hymn "Doch ist es Tag / Sobald man mag / Ein reines Herz dir bringen" (lines 69–71) and the first statement of "Dein Licht, wer will es rauben?" (line 78). And they play a crucial role in strophe 3 (lines 18–27): ascribed by Goethe to a solo male voice from among the pagan populace, this strophe in Mendelssohn's hands is entrusted to "an old woman" from that group (I: mm. 586–627). This strophe is crucial to the plot of the work, for it is precisely the criticism of the naïveté of the druids' initial plans to celebrate their rites "audaciously" that leads to the suggestions that the pagans should post their own sentinels, as well as the subsequent pagan ruse. In Mendelssohn's hands, therefore, the female voices contribute the critical dissenting voice that leads to the pagans' (temporary) victory over their Christian adversaries.

Still other elaborations are more obviously potent as interpretive devices. These elaborations comprise musical cross-references that correlate with or complement those in the poem—thematic and gestural counterparts to the poem's obvious cultivation of repeated words, phrases, and ideas (see "Text and Translation"). In Goethe's poem these conspicuous textual repetitions and varied repetitions serve two functions. Most obviously, they suggest a large-scale responsorial structure: each line, line-pair, or strophe is entrusted first to a solo persona and then to a collective persona; neither ever repeats its own material, and the repeated material is never presented first by the collective and then by a solo. Equally importantly, this almost systematic pattern of repetition emphasizes the text's key structural images and ideas while also enhancing its unity. Mendelssohn's cantata replicates the large-scale solo/collective organization, but it also suggests further metastructures by means of musical recollections. Thus, when the solo druid (tenor) addresses the objections voiced by the old woman "um eurer Sorge Willen" (in order to ease [the] fears [of her and the other women]) the strings restate the staccato string accompaniment that defines her aria "Könnt ihr so verwegen handeln?" (Can you really act so audaciously?) (cf. I: mm. 586–92 and I: mm. 709–13). This musical cross-reference connects these two discrete sections of Part I and makes explicit the dialogic structure of the plot as Goethe wrote it. The original slow introduction to Part II, introducing the Walpurgis Night ruse, restates the  figure from the chorus "Verteilt euch wackre Männer hier" in slow tempo and with somber orchestral timbres, appropriately setting the scene for the nocturnal ruse (cf. I: mm. 744–48 and II: mm. 1–10). The massive deceptive cadence that introduces the instrumental interlude in Part II (II: mm. 388–89) marks not only the beginning of a change of scene from the slopes around the Brocken to the peak itself and the climax of the pagan ruse, but also the culmination of the flickering woodwind turns (example 3) that first appeared with the druid guard's proposal for the hoax (see II: mm. 46–89, passim); as the scene changes this figure recedes into the distance. The fearsome sharply dotted brass interjections, fortissimo, that pervade the Christian guards' panicky music hearken back to their counterpart gestures in the cantata's initial depiction of the pagan solemnities, thus sonically and graphically identifying the source of their fear as "the monsters and the bearded druid with his trombones that stand blasting away behind him" (cf., for example, II: mm. 402–18 and II: mm. 469–72).[59] The same chorus also suggests a kind of mirror image of the relationship between the pagans, the Christians, and the objects of their respective frights: as shown in example 4, the music by which the Christian guards exclaim their fright at witnessing the "Schreckliche, verhexte Leiber / Menschen-Wölf' und Drachen-Weiber" (Horrible, accursed bodies / Human-wolves and dragon-women) clearly parallels that with which the pagan women exclaimed—with far more realistic justification—their horror at seeing their children slaughtered on the tall ramparts of their camp in Part I. Most importantly, most of the music of the pagans' closing hymn is derived from the earlier scene of their sacred rites atop the Blocksberg (cf. II: mm. 421, 522 and II: mm. 450, 528), creating an overarching ternary form whose central section—the Christians' responses to the pagan activities—appears to be of little consequence for the moment.

The last group of Mendelssohn's compositional interventions consists of additions of material implicit in or absent from Goethe's text. These features are at once the most self-evident and the ones most obviously possessed of interpretive implications. The two most prominent such instances are the cantata's extended overture (I: mm. 1–398) and the brief instrumental interlude in Part II (II: mm. 389–401). The first of these compositional additions has attracted considerable attention, for the "bad weather" overture and the ensuing transition to springtime (both instrumental) are at most only implicitly called for by Goethe's poem (the narrative of which begins on Walpurgis Eve, 30 April). Moreover, the length of the overture (398 measures) combines with the complexity and intensity of its music to compel commentary. This is neither a perfunctory A-minor overture nor "a short springtime introduction," but an overtly programmatic symphonic depiction of central Germany's climate during the period preceding the Walpurgis Night—the so-called *Aprilwetter* (April weather), notorious not only for the fury of its inclemency but also for its fickleness.[60] As already discussed, this vivid storm music—evidently the last-conceived part of the music of the 1832–33 version—exposes and develops the core thematic material that will be transformed in the subsequent movements. But it also performs more poetic functions. The tempestuous instability that predominates in the first three hundred bars or

Example 3.

so allegorizes the strife-ridden social and historical context of Goethe's poem. At the same time, in proceeding from that foul weather (emphatically in A minor) to the balmy A-major radiance of springtime, it foreshadows the changes in the pagans' situation over the course of the ballad, from fear and internal dissension to peaceful communal celebration.

The second instrumental episode is required by the narrative of Goethe's ballad but not at all present in its actual structure and content—and if it is in some sense even more audacious than the overture as an interpretive gesture, it is also more perceptive. This episode effectively represents, in the context of an unstaged work, a quasi-operatic diegetic transition—a musical interlude that transports the narrative from one space and one set of dramatis personae to another one. Goethe's text portrays at least three individual or collective personae and three separate spaces. The main groups include the pagan populace as a whole (designated "das Volk" or "the people" by Goethe and Mendelssohn) and their adversaries, the Christian missionaries. The pagans are subdivided into those who celebrate the Walpurgis Night atop the Brocken and the guards who stand watch on the mountain's slopes while the others conduct their rites on high. These two groups occupy different spaces in the narrated story (one group on high and the other standing guard on lower ground), and this space in turn is discrete from that occupied by the Christian guards (who view the pagan ruse from sufficiently far away to be duped into believing that they are observing a single orgiastic and demonic ritual of "human-wolves and female dragons," and indeed Satan himself).

The problem, of course, arose with Mendelssohn's decision to construct his setting of Goethe's poem not as a traditional cantata (i.e., not as a series of self-contained movements separated by short pauses), but as essentially continuous music. With this decision the composer deprived himself of the temporal disruptions that, in conventional cantatas, had permitted differentiations of location and lyric or dramatic personae between movements. As a result, the threefold geographic separation required in strophes 8 through 12—which present *sequentially* the *simultaneous* perspectives of the druid guards still on the territory beneath the peaks (strophes 7 and 8), the other druids atop the Blocksberg (strophes 9 and 12), and the Christians watching both from across the "rocky stretches" (strophes 10 and 11)—require music that somehow accomplishes the effect of a "bleed-through" in staged or filmic theater. To change scene from the druids to their frightened Christian antagonists would have been relatively straightforward, since conventional techniques of musical narrative accounted for such transitions in character delineation. The druids are portrayed by solemn and hymnlike music in C major, and with the

Example 4.

(a) I: 637–42

(b) II: 482–85

move to the Christians the music changes from the previous stately Andante to a *Vivace e con moto* in C minor, with panicky rapid-fire declamation in the solo tenor and scampering and repeated notes in the strings—music evocative of the persecutors' agitation and fright. But the task of differentiating between the two groups of pagans is more complicated because they share a function in the narrative but operate in discrete locations. Some sort of musical mediation was required to prevent this scenic transition from obscuring the geographic separation of the two groups of pagans and thus rendering the narrative unintelligible.

The second instrumental passage accomplishes that transition. Launched by Part II, measure 389, it initially foregrounds the woodwind motive first introduced as the chorus of druid guards begin to accept the solo guard's proposal of a ruse to frighten away the Christians (see II: m. 46). After a final emphatic statement of the chromatic-descent motive (II: mm. 395–96; see example 2, above) and an authentic cadence in A minor (II: mm. 397–98), the thematic and motivic material associated with the pagan ruse begins to give way to the ritual/devotion motive (example 1) as the scene moves to the peak of the Brocken. There, the druid priest laments that he and his people have been forced to worship the *Allvater* secretly and under cover of darkness; in this A-minor intonation the powerful trombone interjections that had emerged as part of the accompaniment beginning in measure 402 come to play an increasingly central role in the thematic and motivic texture, further reinforcing and completing the bleed-through effect.

The Differences between the 1833 and 1844 Versions

The vehemence with which Mendelssohn rejected the early incarnation of *Die erste Walpurgisnacht* after he had completed the overhauled version clearly reflects profound differences between the two. Rather than depriving the early incarnation of its own circumstantially imparted compositional authority, however, it suggests that significant insights into both versions may be gained by comparing them to each other. For convenience, table 1 identifies the passages from the original version that were retained in the final version published as Mendelssohn's opus 60.

The most obvious differences occur in the organization of the two settings—namely in the length of their respective constituent parts. In the version of 1832–33, the overture comprised three sections spanning 398 measures,[61] whereas in the version of 1842–44 (opus 60) it comprises two sections spanning 419 measures. The texted portion of the 1832–33 version is arranged in two metamovements, each comprising six strophes of Goethe's poem, whereas the texted portion of opus 60 consists of nine continuous movements played without pause, with no larger groupings. The final six strophes in the 1832–33 version originally comprised 645 measures, but these were later reduced to 571 measures—remarkably close to the 544 bars of opus 60. On the whole, the bulk of the revisions affecting organization concerned the texted portions of the work, while those that most affected the length occurred in the overture.

Equally important were the final version's wholesale replacement of the 1832–33 music for strophes 5, 10, and 11 and the extensive rewriting of the music for strophes 1 and 9. Mendelssohn provided no specific explanation for these revisions. One might conjecture, however, that the newly composed music for strophe 5 in the final version ("Wer Opfer heut / Zu bringen scheut") was written to clarify the dramatic relationship between it and strophe 9. Both are assigned to "a druid" in Goethe's poem. But whereas this druid is a tenor—presumably the same one as in "Es lacht der Mai!" (I: mm. 390–470)—in the 1832–33 version of Mendelssohn's cantata, he is a baritone (additionally identified by Mendelssohn as "Der Priester") in the final opus 60 version. Similarly, strophes 10 and 11 may have been rewritten to clarify their implied scenic and dramatic context. These strophes adopt the perspective of the terrified Christian guards, identified in the 1832–33 score as a *kleinerer Chor* (smaller chorus) as they observe the monsters and the mysterious flames and lights atop the Brocken from a distance. The 1832–33 version implies the latter spectacle through its prominent and insistent low-brass outbursts but provides little or no clear musical recollection of the monsters so vividly characterized in the preceding "Kommt mit Zacken" chorus. The opus 60 version, by contrast, is suffused with

TABLE 1
Organizational Concordance between 1832–33 and 1843–44 Versions of *Die erste Walpurgisnacht*

Strophe of Poem	Setting of 1832–33	Setting of 1843–44 (Op. 60)
(Overture: "Das schlechte Wetter")	I: mm. 1–340	Overture: mm. 1–359
(Overture, continued: "Der Übergang zum Frühling")*	I: mm. 341–98	Overture: mm. 360–419
1	I: mm. 399–479	No. 1: mm. 1–85
2	I: mm. 480–585	No. 1: mm. 86–220
3	I: mm. 586–636	No. 2: mm. 1–48
4	I: mm. 637–67	No. 2: mm. 49–83
5	I: mm. 668–743	No. 3: mm. 1–44 (NB: music newly composed)
6	I: mm. 744–818	No. 4: mm. 1–73
(instrumental introduction)	II: mm. 1–10	(no counterpart)
7	II: mm. 11–89	No. 5: mm. 1–77
8	II: mm. 90–388	No. 6: mm. 1–306
(instrumental transition)	II: mm. 389–401	No. 7: mm. 1–20
9	II: mm. 402–59	No. 7: mm. 21–71
10	II: mm. 460–81	No. 8: mm. 1–13 (NB: music newly composed)
11	II: mm. 482–516	No. 8: mm. 14–47 (NB: music newly composed)
12	II: mm. 517–71	No. 9: mm. 1–43

* The title "Overture" and the programmatic headings do not appear in the sources of the 1832–33 version, but they are nevertheless implicit.

musical reminiscences of the horrifying spectacle the Christian guards observe (see example 5). The later version thus offers a more vivid musical dramatization of the scene.

The cantata's protracted revision history also reveals some significant practical changes. In the early version the women's chorus adheres largely to the limited and supporting role prescribed by Goethe's poem, but in the final version it participates almost on an equal basis with the men's chorus. Similarly, although Mendelssohn's correspondence reveals that he was considering whether to use bass drum and piccolo already in April 1831, he opted against them in the early version: they are not specified in the score, and no contemporary commentaries allude to them. The issue evidently still troubled him when he returned to the work in the 1840s: the main autograph score for the revised version (see under *AS2* in the "sources" section of the critical report) likewise makes no reference to the piccolo and bass drum, but sometime between December 1842 and February 1843 Mendelssohn thought better of the matter. At that point he wrote out a separate score for piccolo, three trombones, bass drum, and cymbals for the "Kommt mit Zacken" chorus (no. 6 and the beginning of no. 7 of the final version, corresponding to II: mm. 90–402 of this edition). Typical of Mendelssohn's revision process, there are also many cuts and revisions in the orchestration and part-writing.[62]

To interpret the changes between the early and late settings of Goethe's ballad as responses to criticisms and difficulties that had arisen directly in connection with the earlier version is awkward, for most of the changes in the later version have little to do with the issues voiced in contemporary criticisms of the earlier one: the length of the instrumental introduction and of the whole, a supposed lack of vocal cantilena, and a supposedly overindulgent harmonic language. Why, then, could Mendelssohn in 1843 no longer bear "even to think that anyone knows [the *Walpurgisnacht*] in its first version"?

Definitive answers to this question are impossible. Most likely is that the work's early incarnation neither fully represented Mendelssohn's stylistic tendencies as they existed in the 1840s nor addressed his current compositional concerns with the maturity and accomplishment to which he and the public had by then become accustomed. Certainly the sophistication and poised brilliance of opus 60 are consistent with those of the A-minor Symphony, the E-minor Violin Concerto, and the late choral masterpieces, but this line of reasoning also corroborates the artistic validity of the 1832–33 version of the *Walpurgisnacht*. For as Christoph Hellmundt has already argued, the differences between that version and its later counterpart are so extensive, so substantive, and so chronologically discrete that the earlier incarnation clearly qualifies as an autonomous version *(Fassung)*. And that version, after all, was performed publicly as well as privately, acquiring an established musical identity long before Mendelssohn submitted the score and parts for publication.[63] Moreover, however unsatisfactory Mendelssohn may have found the early version a decade later, it nevertheless bespeaks his ideas, interpretive responses to the poem, and professional stance as these existed in the early 1830s, as he prepared and

Example 5. Pan-diegetic material in final version of *Die erste Walpurgisnacht*, op. 60: strophe 10 (no. 8, mm. 2–11).

launched his independent career. Last but not least, the young composer who produced that early version was one whose musical compositions had already established a record for brilliance and integrity. The musical voice that speaks in the pages of the 1832–33 version of *Die erste Walpurgisnacht* is the same voice we find in the *Midsummer Night's Dream* and *Hebrides* Overtures, the D-minor and A-major Symphonies, and of course *St. Paul.*

A Word on the Appendices

Those who study or perform the first version of Mendelssohn's *Die erste Walpurgisnacht* are by definition immersing themselves in his compositional process. That act is by no means merely an academic exercise or an indulgence in curiosities or trivia, however. On the contrary, it is similar to studying or performing the familiar versions of the A-major *(Italian)* and D-minor "Reformation" Symphonies—musical texts that the composer never released for publication (and, in the case of the familiar version of the *Italian* Symphony, for which he later provided an alternative version that he found more satisfactory).[64] The arbiters that evidently make it possible for modern interpreters to override Mendelssohn's rejection of these works are those of circumstance and musical quality—the fact that the first complete version of the *Italian* Symphony and the final version of the *Reformation* Symphony were, at their respective given points, publicly performed under his direction and subsequently with his implicit permission, and that both are imposing musical compositions in their own right. Armed with the circumstantially imparted authority derived from his presentation of these symphonies in public venues, latter-day interpreters regularly treat these works as representative of Mendelssohn's compositional persona, thereby contravening his ultimate decisions to withhold them from print and suppress them entirely. And crucial to these decisions is a belief that the musical quality of the works warrants overriding the composer's own assessment of their success in realizing his intentions. Indeed, how else would one justify posterity's canonization of the *Reformation* Symphony—of all Mendelssohn's works, the one that he declared he would most like to see burned?[65]

This same sort of circumstantially imparted authority and high musical quality also applies to the first version of the *Walpurgisnacht*—a work that is exactly contemporaneous with the A-major and D-minor symphonies, and that he publicly submitted as the finale to the series of concerts he gave as he made his first public bid for his career as a public composer/performer. Moreover, since most or perhaps all of the versions of the *Walpurgisnacht* transmitted in the surviving manuscripts possess some measure of circumstantially imparted authority, the appendices to this edition acknowledge most of these interim variants; only passages that were deleted "on the fly" (i.e., deleted before Mendelssohn moved on to the next measure) are not represented here. The main body of the edition provides a cross-reference to the appropriate appendix at the corresponding point. The text-genetic remarks in the critical notes discuss these variants and, where possible, their respective dates of completion and deletion. Because of the densely recursive revision process within *AS1*, even the deleted measures often contain two or more layers of alteration. Unless otherwise noted, the appendices to this edition give the latest reading of the deleted measures prior to their excision. If the excision also had an effect on the surrounding measures, the respective earlier versions of these measures have been restored and included with the appendices.

Notes

1. Unfortunately, these critical years of Mendelssohn's personal and professional growth have been treated poorly in most biographies. For an accurate, detailed, and vivid account see R. Larry Todd, *Mendelssohn: A Life in Music* (Oxford: Oxford University Press, 2003), 264–417.

2. Until quite recently Mendelssohn's biographers remained largely oblivious to the progressive and innovative values that led his contemporaries to prize his modernity. For new, vivid and historically well-founded accounts that convey a clear sense of his contemporary reception, see especially Clive Brown, *A Portrait of Mendelssohn* (New Haven: Yale University Press, 2003).

3. Translated from the official court history known as the Royal Frankish Annals *(Annales regni Francorum);* see Bernhard Walter Scholz and Barbara Rogers, ed. and trans., *Carolingian Chronicles: Royal Frankish Annals and Nithard's "Histories"* (Ann Arbor: University of Michigan Press, 1972), 51.

4. Translated from [Friedrich Maurer], "Der Brocken," *Berlinisches Archiv der Zeit und ihres Geschmacks* 2 (1796): 535–37. Except where otherwise noted, all translations are my own. For the complete text of Maurer's explanation, along with other contemporary efforts to identify the night's historical origins, see my *Mendelssohn, Goethe, and the Walpurgis Night: The Heathen Muse in Europe, 1700–1850,* Eastman Studies in Music, vol. 43 (New York: University of Rochester Press, 2007), 1–29.

5. "In den letzten Zeiten des Heidenthums in Deutschland, wurden von den Christen die Opfer der Druiden bei Todesstrafe untersagt. Trotz dem suchten die Druiden und das Volk zu Anfang des Frühlings die Höhen der Berge zu gewinnen, dort ihre Opfer zu bringen, und die christlichen Krieger (gewöhnlich durch deren Furcht vor dem Teufel) einzuschüchtern und zu verjagen. Auf solche Versuche soll sich die Sage von der ersten Walpurgisnacht gründen." Programs containing this explanatory note were used in Leipzig for the premiere of the revised version on 2 February 1843 and a performance shortly after Mendelssohn's death, on 11 December 1847. I wish to thank Peter Ward Jones, head of the Music Section of the Bodleian Library, for his assistance in locating and examining the Bodleian's exemplars of these programs.

6. Goethe to Mendelssohn, 9 September 1831, translated from Christoph Hellmundt, "Mendelssohns Arbeit an seiner Kantate *Die erste Walpurgisnacht:* Zu einer bisher wenig beachteten Quelle," in *Felix Mendelssohn Bartholdy: Kongreß-Bericht Berlin 1994,* ed. Christian Martin Schmidt (Wiesbaden: Breitkopf & Härtel, 1997), 105.

7. Zelter to Goethe, 18–21 November 1812, in *Briefwechsel zwischen Goethe und Zelter in den Jahren 1799 bis 1832,* ed. Hans-Günter Ottenberg et al., vol. 20.1 of Johann Wolfgang Goethe, *Sämtliche Werke nach Epochen seines Schaffens, Münchener Ausgabe,* ed. Karl Richter et al. (Munich: Karl Hanser, 1991), 291–93.

8. Goethe to Zelter, 3 December 1812, translated from *Goethes Briefe, Hamburger Ausgabe in 4 Bänden,* ed. Karl Robert Mandelkow, 3rd ed. (Munich: C. H. Beck, 1986), 3:215–16.

9. Mendelssohn to Franz Hauser, March 1831, quoted from Eduard Hanslick, "Aus dem Leben und der Correspondenz von Franz Hauser," in his *Suite: Aufsätze über Musik und Musiker* (Vienna: K. Prochaska, 1884), 26.

10. Emil Bendemann (1807–82), brother of the painter Eduard Bendemann, also a close friend of the composer. I wish to thank Prof. Christian Martin Schmidt for assistance in identifying this "Emil."

11. Mendelssohn to his family in Berlin, 22 February 1831, letter held in the Bodleian Library, Oxford (MS MDM d. 13, fol. 40–41). The German text is reprinted in numerous sources with abridgments and other inaccuracies. A reliable transcription is available in Hellmundt, "Mendelssohns Arbeit," 101.

12. Mendelssohn to Goethe, 5 March 1831, translated from Hellmundt, "Mendelssohns Arbeit," 102.

13. Mendelssohn to his family, 29 March 1831, translated from Hellmundt, "Mendelssohns Arbeit," 102.

14. The Brocken is also commonly referred to as the Blocksberg, a term used for many of Europe's summits.

15. Mendelssohn to his family, 27 April 1831, translated from Hellmundt, "Mendelssohns Arbeit," 102. The 1833 version includes neither bass drum nor piccolo, and the instruments are also absent in the main body of the autograph score for the 1843 revision. A separate score for those instruments as well as trom-

bones in no. 9 shows that they were an afterthought to the later version, included as Mendelssohn prepared the revised version for its premiere.

16. Mendelssohn to his family, 10 May 1831, translated from Hellmundt, "Mendelssohns Arbeit," 103.

17. See Ibid.

18. Translated Ibid. The introduction of "[X]" and "[Y]," which are absent from the original, was necessary because the sentence structure of the original cannot be preserved in English: "Aber nun da es fertig vor mir liegt, sehe ich daß es zu einem großen Concertstück sehr gut paßt und in meinem ersten Abonnementsconcert in Berlin mußt Du den bärtigen Druidenpriester singen, die Chöre ausgeführt von, unter gütiger Mitwirkung des etc."

19. Translated from Hellmundt, "Mendelssohns Arbeit," 104.

20. Diary entry for 17 July 1831 reads: "Sonntag. 17 Arb[eit] Walp[urgisnacht] fertig geputzt" (Sunday the 17th. Work. Finished tidying up the Walpurgisnacht). See Hellmundt, "Mendelssohns Arbeit," 104.

21. Carl Thomas Mozart (1784–1858); oldest son of Wolfgang Amadeus and Constanze Mozart. See Hellmundt, "Mendelssohns Arbeit," 104. For an explanation of the source sigla (*AS1, AS2, APf1,* etc.) used in this introduction, see "Sources" in the critical report.

22. Mendelssohn to Eduard Devrient, 27 August 1831. The high F in question is presumably the one given in m. 521 of Part II, just a few pages from the end of the 1832–33 composing score (see under *AS1* in the "Sources" section of the critical report).

23. Mendelssohn to Goethe, 28 August 1831, translated from Hellmundt, "Mendelssohns Arbeit," 105.

24. Goethe's phrase "hoch symbolisch" is usually translated as "highly symbolic." This translation is misleading, however, for the German phrase refers not to the degree of symbolism—as, for example, "sehr symbolisch" or "höchst symbolisch" would, and as the English phrase does—but to the nature of the symbolic intent.

25. Goethe to Mendelssohn, 9 September 1831, translated from Hellmundt, "Mendelssohns Arbeit," 105.

26. Mendelssohn to Fanny Hensel, 21 January 1832, and entry of 4 February 1832 in an unpublished diary held in the Staatsbibliothek zu Berlin–Preußischer Kulturbesitz (Mendelssohn-Archiv, shelfmark MA Ms. 143). See Hellmundt, "Mendelssohns Arbeit," 106.

27. Mendelssohn to his family, 13 February 1832, translated from Hellmundt, "Mendelssohns Arbeit," 106–7. Precisely what Mendelssohn meant by "the seven movements" is unclear. Goethe's poem is cast in twelve stanzas; the extant sources of the 1832–33 setting of the cantata organizes these into two large-scale numbers (introducing and depicting the Walpurgis Night, respectively); the autograph for the 1843–44 revision recognizes ten movements, counting the overture as no. 1, and the final version published as opus 60 recognizes nine movements, beginning its numbering with the first strophe. The musical organization of Mendelssohn's 1832–33 setting and the poem's pattern of solo–chorus–counter-solo–counter-chorus suggest the following possibility: no. 1 = strophes 1–2; no. 2 = strophes 3–4; no. 3 = strophes 5–6; no. 4 = strophes 7–8; no. 5 = strophe 9; no. 6 = strophes 10–11; no. 7 = strophe 12.

28. But see also the remarks under "Notes on Performance"on the private performance given in Berlin in October 1832, below.

29. See his sharp-tongued but clear-headed assessment in his letter written on 16 September 1832 to Franz Hauser, quoted in Wolfgang Dinglinger, "Felix Mendelssohn Bartholdys Berliner Intermezzo," *Mendelssohn-Studien* 13 (2003): 108. See also Wm. A. Little, "Mendelssohn and the Berlin Singakademie: The Composer at the Crossroads," in *Mendelssohn and His World*, ed. R. Larry Todd (Princeton: Princeton University Press, 1991), 65–85.

30. See Dinglinger, "Berliner Intermezzo," 116–20. The third concert was originally slated and advertised for 20 December 1832, but it had to be postponed because of mounting difficulties, including the illness of Eduard Devrient.

31. Mendelssohn to his family, 22 February 1831, and Charlotte Moscheles, *Aus Moscheles' Leben: Nach Briefen und Tagebüchern* (Leipzig: Duncker & Humblot, 1872–73), 1:252.

32. Translation quoted from Little, "Mendelssohn and the Berlin Singakademie," 77.

33. Rellstab's review (untitled) of Mendelssohn's concert of 15 November 1832, *Vossische Zeitung* 271 (17 November 1832), translated from Dinglinger, "Berliner Intermezzo," 118.

34. Louis Spohr, *Faust,* romantic opera in two acts, on a libretto by J. C. Bernard (composed in 1813, premiered in 1816, and published in 1822); Weber, *Der Freischütz,* romantic opera in three acts, on a libretto by Friedrich Kind (composed in 1817–21 and premiered and published in 1821).

35. *Königlich privilegirte Berlinische Zeitung von Staats- und gelehrten Sachen* 10 (12 January 1833): [6–7]; translated from Hellmundt, "Mendelssohns Arbeit," 108–9.

36. Translated from Hellmundt, "Mendelssohns Arbeit," 109.

37. A double entendre meaning both "the bulk of the public" and "the coarser parts of the public."

38. Lea Mendelssohn Bartholdy to Ferdinand David, mid-January 1833; translated from Dinglinger, "Berliner Intermezzo," 121.

39. The two movements of the 1832–33 version comprise the beginning through no. 4 and nos. 5–9 of opus 60. To avoid confusion with the designated movements in the later setting, this text refers to those in the early setting as Part I and Part II. In describing the revisions to Hensel on 13 January 1843, Mendelssohn stated that his older sister "knew the earlier version better than anyone but [himself]." In response, Hensel wrote back on 17 January with a clear reference to her having performed the role of "Eine alte Frau"; see note 52, below.

40. See Fanny Hensel, *Tagebücher,* ed. Hans-Günter Klein and Rudolf Elvers (Wiesbaden: Breitkopf & Härtel, 2002), 41.

41. Ibid., 42.

42. Hensel to Mendelssohn, ca. 27–28 February 1834, translated and quoted in *The Letters of Fanny Hensel to Felix Mendelssohn,* ed. Marcia J. Citron ([Stuyvesant, N.J.]: Pendragon, 1987), 128 and 456.

43. *The Letters of Fanny Hensel to Felix Mendelssohn,* 192 and 503; 198 and 507.

44. Mendelssohn to Fanny Hensel, 7 April 1834, translated from *Fanny und Felix Mendelssohn, "Die Musik will gar nicht rutschen ohne Dich": Briefwechsel 1821 bis 1846,* ed. Eva Weissweiler (Berlin: Propyläen, 1997), 160 (original in New York Public Library, no. 186).

45. The concert for which the cantata was mentioned was given on 3 May, without it.

46. See my *Mendelssohn, Goethe, and the Walpurgis Night,* 87–88 and 115–16.

47. Mendelssohn to Karl Klingemann, 18 November 1840, translated from *Felix Mendelssohn Bartholdys Briefwechsel mit Legationsrat Karl Klingemann in London,* ed. Karl Klingemann, [jr.] (Essen: G. D. Baedecker, 1909), 251.

48. Mendelssohn to Lea Mendelssohn Bartholdy, 28 November 1842, translated from Hellmundt, "Mendelssohns Arbeit," 110.

49. See Hellmundt, "Mendelssohns Arbeit," 78.

50. Mendelssohn to Rebecka Dirichlet (his younger sister), 11 December 1842, held in the New York Public Library (no. 531). Excerpts from this letter have been printed in numerous collections with the addressee erroneously identified as Lea Mendelssohn Bartholdy. See, for example, *Briefe aus den Jahren 1833 bis 1847 von Felix Mendelssohn Bartholdy,* ed. Paul and Carl Mendelssohn Bartholdy (Leipzig: Hermann Mendelssohn, 1863), 356–58.

51. Mendelssohn to Fanny Hensel, Leipzig, 13 January 1843, translated from Hellmundt, "Mendelssohns Arbeit," 110.

52. Hensel to Mendelssohn, 17 January 1843, translated with minor emendations from *The Letters of Fanny Hensel to Felix Mendelssohn,* 314. For the original German, see *The Letters of*

Fanny Hensel to Felix Mendelssohn, 587; and Hellmundt, "Mendelssohns Arbeit," 111.

53. For a more detailed reconstruction of these complicated final stages and the extensive revisions they entailed, see chapters 4 and 5 of my *Mendelssohn, Goethe, and the Walpurgis Night.*

54. The *Voyage musicale* was published in French and German later in 1843 and then reprinted, with further annotations, in Berlioz's *Memoirs* in 1866. In the *Memoirs* Berlioz added a footnote stating that he "had not then heard his ravishing *Midsummer Night's Dream.*" See *The Memoirs of Hector Berlioz, Member of the French Institute, Including His Travels in Italy, Germany, Russia, and England, 1803–1865,* ed. and trans. David Cairns, corrected edition (New York: W. W. Norton, 1975), 294.

55. *The Memoirs of Hector Berlioz,* 294.

56. "Z" [Oswald Lorenz], *Neue Zeitschrift für Musik* 18 (1843): 67–68.: "... ein außerordentlich schönes Ding, eine Cantata, oder Ballade will er's lieber nennen. Ich habe lange nicht so etwas gesundes und frisches gehört, was einem so das Herz erfreute."

57. Henceforth, parenthetical references to specific measures identify the part no. in roman numerals and the measure(s) in arabic numerals (e.g., I: m. 100 refers to measure 100 in Part I).

58. See also Douglass Seaton, "The Romantic Mendelssohn: the Composition of *Die erste Walpurgisnacht,*" *Musical Quarterly* 68 (1982): 398–410, esp. 406–10.

59. Mendelssohn to his family, 14 July 1831, translated from Hellmundt, "Mendelssohns Arbeit," 104.

60. See Thomas Grey, "The Orchestral Music," in *The Mendelssohn Companion,* ed. Douglass Seaton, 395–550 (Westport, Conn.: Greenwood, 2001), 498–503; and especially Juliette Laurence Appold, *Landschaften in Mendelssohns Briefen, Bildern und Kompositionen* (Essen: Die blaue Eule, 2007), esp. part II, chapter 4 (pp. 110–36) (originally Ph.D. dissertation, Philipps-Universität Marburg, 2005).

61. Mendelssohn to Klingemann, Leipzig, 18 November 1840 (cited in note 47).

62. See Hellmundt, "Mendelssohns Arbeit;" Peter Krause, "Mendelssohns dramatische Kantate *Die erste Walpurgisnacht:* Ergänzende Bemerkungen zur Werkgeschichte auf der Grundlage von Untersuchungen des Leipziger Autographs der Letztfassung," in *Musik + Dramaturgie: 15 Studien Fritz Hennenberg zum 65. Geburtstag,* ed. Beate Hiltner-Hennenberg (Frankfurt am Main: Peter Lang, 1997), 101–21; Hiromi Hoshino, "Ein neu-entdecktes Mendelssohn-Autograph in Japan: Der Klavierauszug 'Die erste Walpurgisnacht,' op. 60," *Die Musikforschung* 57 (2004): 151–59; and chapter 5 of my *Mendelssohn, Goethe, and the Walpurgis Night.*

63. See Hellmundt, "Mendelssohns Arbeit," 99–100.

64. The D-minor Symphony was composed in 1830–32, rehearsed in Paris early in 1832, and premiered in an overhauled version under Mendelssohn's direction in Berlin on 15 November 1832. It was further performed under the direction of his close friend Julius Rietz in Düsseldorf on 12 December 1837, but Mendelssohn withheld it from publication; the first edition appeared in 1868, more than twenty years after his death. The first version of the A-major Symphony was completed in the spring of 1833 and premiered under Mendelssohn's direction on 13 May of that year, but in June 1834 he thoroughly rewrote the last three movements, stating that he had stumbled upon "so many *errata*" in the earlier version of those movements that he decided to recompose them wholesale (Mendelssohn to Ignaz Moscheles, 26 June 1834). This symphony, too, Mendelssohn withheld from print. The first edition, published posthumously in 1848, was prepared without evident awareness or consultation of the revised version of the last three movements. The revised version was first published in 2001 by Ludwig-Reichert-Verlag (Wiesbaden). For a review of this situation and the complete correspondence concerning the revision of the A-major Symphony, see my *Mendelssohn's "Italian" Symphony* (Oxford: Oxford University Press, 2003), 33–45.

65. Letter of 11 February 1838 to Julius Rietz, held in the Library of Congress, Washington, D.C., and frequently reprinted. See Wolfgang Dinglinger, "The Programme of Mendelssohn's 'Reformation' Symphony," in *The Mendelssohns: Their Music in History,* ed. John Michael Cooper and Julie D. Prandi, 115–33 (Oxford: Oxford University Press, 2002), 130–33.

Notes on Performance

As explained in the critical report, this edition is based primarily on the holograph full score held in the Biblioteka Jagiellońska, Kraków, Poland. Since this autograph was not submitted for publication during Mendelssohn's lifetime, it is best viewed as a composing score that transmits the cantata as a work-in-progress. In particular, it evidently reflects most of the revisions—small and large—in Mendelssohn's conception of the work between late 1830 and at least January 1833.[1] Moreover, since the autograph transmits a musical text that reflects specific assumptions and circumstances of musical performance, its musical notation offers a particularly graphic picture of the intersection of compositional conception and realization in performance. In other words, the autograph documents the genesis and metamorphosis of *Die erste Walpurgisnacht* not only in the compositional sense, but also with regard to practical performance. In order to empower modern interpreters to make their own informed decisions, this edition aims to facilitate a comparably clear image of the work's evolution in composition and performance, presenting the most significant revisions and deletions in a series of appendices following the main score.

The complete early version of *Die erste Walpurgisnacht* was performed three times during Mendelssohn's lifetime: privately in London on 30 April 1832, in Hensel's Sunday musicale on 11 October 1832, and in the public premiere given in Berlin on 10 January 1833. The circumstances of the last-named are reasonably clear (see the discussion under "Chronology," in the introduction), but those of the private performances remain ambiguous. The autograph piano-duet arrangement of the "bad weather" overture (see Appendix III and the discussion of source *APf1* in the critical report) suggests that the composer may have realized the secondo part for that section, while someone else played the primo part.[2] In accordance with nineteenth-century customs for such matters, the person who initially played the primo part would then have moved to the podium to direct the chorus for the remainder of the work, leaving the original secondo player to accompany the remainder from the keyboard. Given Mendelssohn's well-documented and prodigious musical memory,[3] it is entirely possible that he performed as secondo/solo accompanist in the private performance of November 1832. Moreover, we may securely conjecture that the role of primo/conductor was taken by Fanny Hensel in this performance, since the siblings' correspondence documents her intimate familiarity with the work.

Tempo

Mendelssohn provided precise tempo and metronome markings for the published editions of the final version of *Die erste Walpurgisnacht*. These markings, given in the orchestral score, the German and English piano/vocal arrangement, and the choral parts, were entered sometime between the completion of the respective autographs and the appearance of the editions themselves. Those whose music has a clear counterpart in the version of 1832–33 are as displayed in table 1.

Roles and Casting

Aside from the names and voice-types of the soloists in the performance given on 10 January 1833, little information survives concerning these aspects of the documented performances of the first version. The following information may be gleaned from the autograph score for this version in tandem with the autograph score and piano/vocal arrangement for the final version, contemporary concert programs, and the first editions:

1. The program should identify the dramatis personae in the manner customary in productions of operas (after the information provided on p. 2 of this volume).

2. Goethe's poem indicates that strophe 3 ("Könnt ihr so verwegen handeln?") should be sung by "Einer aus dem Volk" (literally, a man from among the people). Nevertheless, all three of Mendelssohn's autograph scores that include his setting of this strophe *(AS1, AS2,* and *APf2)* identify this role as "Eine alte Frau" (an old woman). The program for the premiere of the final version (2 February 1843) identifies this role as "Eine Frau aus dem Volke" (a woman from among the people), and the first German edition of the printed score specifies "Eine alte Frau aus dem Volke. Alto Solo."

3. The sources raise some questions regarding the casting of the male soloists. All three autograph scores *(AS1, AS2,* and *APf2)* assign the roles of the druid in strophe 1 ("Es lacht der Mai!") and the Christian guard in strophe 10 ("Hilf, ach hilf mir, Kriegsgeselle") to tenor solo, i.e., they are to be sung by a tenor in both the

Table 1
Metronome Marks from 1843–44 Version (Opus 60) as Applicable to 1832–33 Version

Section	Measures	Metronome Mark
No. 1: Einleitung		
Overture, section 1 ("Das schlechte Wetter")	1–340	𝅗𝅥. = 60
Overture, section 2 ("Übergang zum Frühling")	341–98	𝅗𝅥 = 96
Strophe 1	399–479	𝅗𝅥 = 96
Strophe 2	480–585	𝅗𝅥 = 160
Strophes 3 and 4	586–667	♩ = 80
Strophe 5	668–743	no counterpart in op. 60
Strophe 6	744–818	𝅗𝅥 = 88
No. 2		
Instrumental introduction	1–10	no counterpart in op. 60
Strophe 7, lines 50–53	11–14	Recitativo $\frac{3}{4}$
Strophe 7, repeat of lines 52–53	15–20	♩ = 104
Strophe 7, lines 54–59	21–90	♩ = 144
Strophe 8	91–388	𝅗𝅥. = 88
Instrumental interlude	389–401	♩ = 88*
Strophe 9	402–59	♩ = 72
Strophes 10 and 11	460–516	no counterpart in op. 60
Strophe 12	517–71	♩ = 80

* The actual metronome mark in the 1844 version is 𝅗𝅥 = 88, but note values are doubled compared to the 1833 version.

1832–33 and 1842–44 versions, but in the 1832–33 version strophes 5 and 7 ("Wer Opfer heut / Zu bringen scheut" and "Diese dumpfen Pfaffenchristen") are also written for tenor, rather than for the bass-baritone solo used for these two strophes, strophe 10, and strophe 12 in the final version (op. 60). Moreover, page 106/113 of the autograph full score for the 1832–33 version (source *AS1*) specifies that strophe 10 is to be sung by a different tenor solo ("Tenore Solo 2ndo"). The sources for the two versions thus suggest the role-assignments displayed in table 2 for the version of 1832–33.

4. Similar problems occur with regard to the choruses. In view of the plot of the cantata, the specifications provided by the autographs and the first editions suggest that the chorus should be divided into two groups, with the men on one side of the stage and the women on the other. The male choruses in strophes 2, 6, 7, and 11 might comprise different subsets (each TTBB) of the former, while the "Chor der Weiber" might comprise the smaller women's chorus drawn from what in this edition is called the "Chor des Heidenvolks." Only in strophes 8, 9, and 12 (II: mm. 91–459 and II: mm. 517–71) does it seem likely that the entire choir should be used.[4] At the same time, performers might consider the sort of choral distribution employed by Berlioz in his *Roméo et Juliette*.[5]

Ensemble Issues

Mendelssohn's contemporaries consistently noted two aspects of his orchestration: its capacity for expressive nuance and its capacity for achieving richness and grandeur without at the same time becoming muddy or unwieldy. The observations are hardly surprising, given his extensive experience both within and at the helm of orchestral and orchestral/choral ensembles.[6] They also reflect the intimate connection between his orchestration and the instruments and orchestral conventions of his day. And they certainly account for his extraordinary effectiveness as a conductor who consistently delivered what were by most accounts highly personalized and nuanced readings of his own works as well as compositions by other composers from the early seventeenth century through his own day.

What all this means for latter-day performers is that the music benefits from an intimate familiarity with the timbres, tempos, and approaches to phrasing that were operative in Mendelssohn's imagination as he wrote. Performers respond substantively and intuitively to the tactile, timbral, and structural features of their individual instruments and the circumstances in which they are used. These same factors also affect composers' decisions concerning notation, voicing, phrasing, fingering, etc. Whether historical instruments or modern ones are used, an understanding of the circumstances and sounds that Mendelssohn envisioned can only enrich and enliven the interpretation.[7]

The extensive body of primary sources that surround Mendelssohn's life and creative work tell us that *Die erste Walpurgisnacht* took shape in Munich and Milan; that the overture was written in Paris; and that the work was publicly premiered in Berlin. We may also reasonably conjecture that Mendelssohn's conducting triumphs in London in 1829 and 1832 tempered his ideas on orchestral conducting. Although the sizes and dispositions of orchestral and orchestral/choral ensembles in these locations were not entirely consistent, they concur in several

TABLE 2

Role Assignments in *Die erste Walpurgisnacht:* Correspondence between the 1832–33 and 1843–44 Versions

Strophe	1832–33*		1843–44	
1	Ein Druide [1]	Tenor [1]	Ein Druide	Tenor
			Chor des Volkes	SATB
2	Ein Druide [1]	Tenor [1]	Ein Druide	Tenor
	Chor der Druiden	TTBB	Chor der Druiden und des Volkes	SATB
3	Eine alte Frau	Alto	Eine alte Frau aus dem Volke	Alto
4	Eine alte Frau	Alto	Eine alte Frau aus dem Volke	Alto
	Chor der Weiber	SSAA	Chor der Weiber aus dem Volke	SSAA
5	Ein Druide [1]	Tenor [1]	Der Priester der Druiden	Baritone
			Chor der Druiden	TTBB
6	(unnamed chorus)	TTBB	Chor der Wächter der Druiden	SATB
7	Ein Druide [1]	Tenor [1]	Ein Wächter der Druiden	Bass
	(unnamed chorus)	TTBB	Chor der Wächter der Druiden	TTBB
8	(unnamed chorus)	SATB	Chor der Wächter der Druiden und des Heidenvolks	SATB
9	Ein Druide [2]	Baritone	Der Priester der Druiden	Baritone
	Chor der Männer	TTBB	Chor der Druiden und des Heidenvolks	SATB
10	Ein Wächter	Tenor 2	Ein christlicher Wächter	Tenor
11			Ein christlicher Wächter	Tenor
	Chor der Wächter (kleinerer Chor)	TTBB	Chor der christlichen Wächter	TTBB
12	Ein Druide [2]	Baritone	Der Priester der Druiden	Baritone
	Chor der Druiden (Frauenchor / Der ganze Männerchor)	SATB	Chor der Druiden und des Heidenvolks	SATB

* In this table the labels for the 1832–33 version appear as in *AS1* and are not regularized. For the edited labels as used in this edition, as well as English translations, see table of contents and "Text and Translation."

key aspects. First, the strings, winds, and voices alike treated vibrato as an ornament to be selectively employed for emphasis on particular notes or passages, not a staple of tone.[8] Second, their orchestras were considerably smaller than the latter-day norm: all used doubled winds and one player to a part on the brass parts (still the norm in modern ensembles), but the string sections were considerably smaller, with twenty-five to twenty-nine violins.[9] Third, the seating arrangements as well as the physical construction of the instruments emphasized heterogeneity and contrast rather than the latter-day norms of blend and bulk. Almost every orchestral ensemble seated the first and second violins across from each other, and English practice also divided the cellos and basses (except that the principals were placed at or near the center). Finally, except for the enormous ensembles used for the outdoor public music festivals, most institutions preferred to place the chorus or choruses in front of the orchestra; the conductor stood between the choral and orchestral ensembles, and his directions were made visible to the choruses at his back by means of assistant conductors and mirrors.[10] On the whole, these performance traditions resulted in a substantially different manner of presentation—one that offered composers and conductors a different set of advantages than those to which modern performers may otherwise be accustomed.

Mendelssohn's ability to explore the dynamic, timbral, textural, and dramatic possibilities offered by these conventions of orchestral practice certainly accounted in no small part for contemporaries' admiration of his orchestration. In the *Walpurgisnacht* as in many other contemporary scores, the finely tuned manipulation of orchestral color praised by his contemporaries is probably reflected in his frequent use of diamond-shaped crescendo/diminuendo hairpins (<>) to prescribe a rather dramatic crescendo followed by a diminuendo that is immediate, not delayed. The different orchestral balances created by the comparatively small body of strings—or, conversely, the higher ratio of winds to strings—permits the detailed wind writing to speak vividly rather than simply complementing the string sound (this is especially true in the overture and strophes 7 and 8). Similarly, the relatively sparing use of the brass becomes all the more dramatic because of the brilliance of the higher notes on period instruments and the comparatively transparent sound of the remainder of the orchestral palette. Chromatic notes that had to be stopped offered another timbral possibility on these instruments (for example, the E-flats and B-naturals in the horns at II: mm. 111–15 and the E-flats at II: mm. 391–94).

Performances in English

For most of the nineteenth century, copyright conventions required that compositions be published simultaneously in at least two, and preferably three, different countries in order to preserve the rights of publication. Mendelssohn's well-documented fluency in English sets the contemporary English editions of his works apart from those of (for example) Haydn and Beethoven. This composer, who visited England ten times between 1829 and 1847, read, wrote, and spoke English fluently (as well as French, classical Greek, and Italian) and maintained extensive ties to England to the end of his career. He was admirably qualified to create, critique, and amend English translations of his music. The English first edition of opus 60 was published with the same text by Mendelssohn's preferred English translator for his works, William Bartholomew. Since Mendelssohn was a competent judge and did approve Bartholomew's English translation in 1843–44, it is also included in this edition, and constitutes a viable option for ensembles that wish to perform the *Walpurgisnacht* in English.

Notes

1. As Hellmundt points out, at least one other significant source can no longer be traced. This autograph transmits an early version of the overture that began with an Andante in G minor before moving to C major or A minor; it was notated before 13 February 1832. It was auctioned by Hans Schneider (Tutzing, Germany) in 1978, probably to a private collector. See Christoph Hellmundt, "Mendelssohns Arbeit an seiner Kantate *Die erste Walpurgisnacht:* Zu einer bisher wenig beachteten Quelle," in *Felix Mendelssohn Bartholdy: Kongreß-Bericht Berlin 1994*, ed. Christian Martin Schmidt (Wiesbaden: Breitkopf & Härtel, 1997), 79.

2. An edition of the autograph piano-duet arrangement of the overture is included as Appendix III in this volume.

3. See Clive Brown, *A Portrait of Mendelssohn* (New Haven: Yale University Press, 2003), 230–35.

4. Of course, the plot of the poem would suggest that the chorus of Christian guards (smaller male chorus) *not* participate in the final chorus, although as a practical matter this would be discernible only if that subchorus were separately positioned (see note 5). See chapter 7 of my *Mendelssohn, Goethe, and the Walpurgis Night: The Heathen Muse in Europe, 1700–1850*, Eastman Studies in Music (New York: University of Rochester Press, 2007), esp. 212–13, for a more detailed discussion of this issue.

5. See Donna M. Di Grazia, "Rejected Traditions: Ensemble Placement in Nineteenth-Century Paris," *Nineteenth-Century Music* 22 (1998): 190–209, esp. 198–200.

6. See Brown, *Portrait*, 235–57.

7. Many writers, mostly proceeding from simplistic readings of Richard Wagner's later writings concerning Mendelssohn's conducting, have misrepresented his conducting and his views on the interpreter's tasks in general. Two recent essays offer essential correctives to this long-standing history: Donald Mintz, "Mendelssohn as Performer and Teacher," in *The Mendelssohn Companion*, ed. Douglass Seaton (Westport, Conn.: Greenwood, 2001), 101–42; and especially Leon Botstein, "Wagner as Mendelssohn: Reversing Habits and Reclaiming Meaning in the Performance of Mendelssohn's Music for Orchestra and Chorus," in *The Cambridge Companion to Mendelssohn*, ed. Peter Mercer-Taylor (Cambridge: Cambridge University Press, 2004), 251–68.

8. See Clive Brown, "Bowing Styles, Vibrato and Portamento in Nineteenth-Century Violin Playing," *Journal of the Royal Musical Association* 113 (1988): 97–128.

9. On these points, see especially chapter 12 ("Concert Seating Plans") in Daniel J. Koury, *Orchestral Performance Practices in the Nineteenth Century: Size, Proportions, Seating* (Ann Arbor, Mich.: UMI Research Press, 1986), 201–37.

10. On this issue—and of critical importance in works such as the *Walpurgisnacht*—see especially Di Grazia, "Rejected Traditions," 190–209. The article centers on Parisian practice, but the convention of placing the chorus at the front of the ensemble was widely practiced on the Continent.

Text and Translation

This chapter renders the libretto as set by Mendelssohn. The composer's departures from Goethe's poem and further editorial interventions are reported in endnotes. The strophes of the poem are not marked in the musical sources, but as in the edition this information has been included here for orientation. William Bartholomew's English translation (1843), intended for performance, does not adhere literally to the German original. Because of this, the editor has provided a new, faithful prose translation. For Bartholomew's version, see the score.

Characters

Ein Druide[1]	A druid
Eine alte Frau[2]	An old woman
Ein christlicher Wächter[3]	A Christian guard
Chor der Druiden	Chorus of druids
Chor der Weiber	Chorus of women
Chor der Wächter des Heidenvolks[4]	Chorus of guards of the pagan people
Chor des Heidenvolks[5]	Chorus of pagan people
Chor der christlichen Wächter[6]	Chorus of Christian guards

No. 1[7]

EINLEITUNG[8]

Ouverture: Das schlechte Wetter – Der Übergang zum Frühling[9]

INTRODUCTION

Overture: Bad Weather—The Transition to Spring

Strophe 1

EIN DRUIDE (1)

Es lacht der Mai!
Der Wald ist frei
Von Eis und Reifgehänge.
Der Schnee ist fort;
Am grünen Ort
Erschallen Luftgesänge.[10]
Ein reiner Schnee
Liegt auf der Höh';
Doch eilen wir nach oben,
Begehn den alten heil'gen Brauch,
Allvater dort zu loben!
Die Flamme lodre durch den Rauch!
So wird das Herz erhoben.

A DRUID

May is laughing!
The forest is free
of ice and hanging hoarfrost,
the snow is gone;
in the green place
merry songs of breezes resound.
A pristine snow
lies on the peak;
let's hasten up there
to celebrate the ancient holy rite,
to praise the father of all.
May the flame blaze through the smoke!
Thus will the heart be edified.

Strophe 2

EIN DRUIDE (1) UND CHOR DER DRUIDEN[11]

Die Flamme lodre durch den Rauch!
Begeht den alten heil'gen Brauch,
Allvater dort zu loben!
Hinauf! Hinauf nach oben!

A DRUID AND CHORUS OF DRUIDS

May the flame blaze through the smoke!
Celebrate the ancient holy rite
there, praising the father of all.
Away! Upward to the heights!

STROPHE 3

EINE ALTE FRAU
Könnt ihr so verwegen handeln?
Wollt ihr denn zum Tode wandeln?
Kennet ihr nicht die Gesetze
Unsrer harten Überwinder?
Rings gestellt sind ihre Netze
Auf die Heiden, auf die Sünder.
Ach, sie schlachten auf dem Walle
Unsre Väter,[12] unsre Kinder.
Und wir alle
Nahen uns gewissem Falle.

AN OLD WOMAN
Can you [really] behave so audaciously?
Do you want to stroll up to death?
Don't you know the laws
of our stubborn conquerors?
Their snares have been set all around
for the pagans, for the sinners.
Ah, on their ramparts they slaughter
our fathers, our children.
And we all
are approaching our certain downfall.

STROPHE 4

CHOR DER WEIBER
Auf des Lagers hohem Walle
Schlachten sie schon unsre Kinder.
Ach, die strengen Überwinder!
Und wir alle
Nahen uns gewissem Falle.

CHORUS OF WOMEN
On the camp's high ramparts
they're already slaughtering our children.
Ah, the stubborn conquerors!
And we all
are approaching our certain downfall.

STROPHE 5

EIN DRUIDE (1)
Wer Opfer heut'
Zu bringen scheut,
Verdient erst seine Bande.
Der Wald ist frei!
Das Holz herbei,
Und schichtet es zum Brande!
Doch bleiben wir
Im Buschrevier
Am Tage noch im Stillen,
Und Männer stellen wir zur Hut
Um eurer Sorge willen.
Dann aber lasst mit frischem Mut
Uns unsre Pflicht erfüllen!

A DRUID
Anyone who shies away
from sacrifice today
has earned his bondage.
The forest is free!
Bring some wood here
and pile it up for a fire!
But we'll remain
in the brushy areas
during the daytime,
and we'll post men as guards
because of your concern.
But then let us fulfill our duty
with renewed zeal!

STROPHE 6

CHOR DER WÄCHTER DES HEIDENVOLKS
Verteilt euch, wackre Männer, hier
Durch dieses ganze Waldrevier
Und wachet hier im stillen,
Wenn sie die Pflicht erfüllen!

CHORUS OF GUARDS OF THE PAGAN PEOPLE
Spread out here, brave men,
all throughout this forest grove,
and keep watch here in the quiet
while they fulfill their [own] duty.

No. 2[13]

STROPHE 7

EIN DRUIDE (1)[14]
Diese dumpfen Pfaffenchristen,
Lasst uns keck sie überlisten!
Mit dem Teufel, den sie fabeln,
Wollen wir sie selbst erschrecken.

A DRUID
These foolish cleric-Christians!
Let's outwit them with cleverness!
Let's frighten them
with their own fabled devil.

EIN DRUIDE (1) UND CHOR DER WÄCHTER DES HEIDENVOLKS
Kommt! Mit Zacken und mit Gabeln
Und mit Glut und Klapperstöcken
Lärmen wir bei nächt'ger Weile
Durch die engen Felsenstrecken.

A DRUID AND CHORUS OF GUARDS OF THE PAGAN PEOPLE
Come! With prongs and pitchforks
and with embers and clappers
let's make a racket during our night-watch
in the narrow rocky stretches.

Kauz und Eule,
Heul' in unser Rundgeheule.

Hoopoe and owl,
howl along with us.

Strophe 8

CHOR DES HEIDENVOLKS

Kommt mit Zacken und mit Gabeln
Wie der Teufel, den sie fabeln,
Und mit wilden Klapperstöcken
Durch die leeren Felsenstrecken.
Kauz und Eule,
Heul' in unser Rundgeheule.

CHORUS OF PAGAN PEOPLE

Come with prongs and pitchforks,
like their fabled devil,
with wild clappers
through the empty rocky stretches!
Hoopoe and owl,
howl along with us.

Strophe 9

EIN DRUIDE (2) UND CHOR DER DRUIDEN[15]

So weit gebracht,
Dass wir bei Nacht
Allvater heimlich singen!
Doch ist es Tag,
Sobald man mag
Ein reines Herz dir bringen.
Du kannst zwar heut'
Und manche Zeit
Dem Feinde viel erlauben.
Die Flamme reinigt sich vom Rauch:
So reinig' unsern Glauben!
Und raubt man uns den alten Brauch:
Dein Licht, wer will es rauben!

A DRUID AND CHORUS OF DRUIDS

So it's come to this:
that we sing to the father of all
Under cover of darkness!
But it is daytime
as soon as one desires
to approach you with a pure heart!
You can allow the enemy
great latitude
today and many a day.
The flame purifies itself of smoke:
thus purify our faith!
And if we are robbed of our ancient rite,
who would rob us of your light!

Strophe 10

EIN CHRISTLICHER WÄCHTER

Hilf, ach hilf mir, Kriegsgeselle!
Ach, es kommt die ganze Hölle!
Sieh, wie die verhexten Leiber
Durch und durch von Flamme glühen!
Menschen-Wölf' und Drachen-Weiber,
Die im Flug vorüberziehen!
Welch entsetzliches Getöse!
Lasst uns, lasst uns alle fliehen!
Oben flammt und saust der Böse;
Aus dem Boden
Dampfet rings ein Höllen-Broden.

A CHRISTIAN GUARD

Help! oh help me, my comrades in war!
Ah, all hell is coming toward us!
Look how the bewitched corpses
glow all over with flame!
Wolf-men and dragon-women
fly about overhead!
What a terrible ruckus!
Let us—let's all flee!
Up above the Evil One flames,
out of the earth
a hellish broth boils up around us.

Strophe 11

EIN CHRISTLICHER WÄCHTER UND CHOR DER CHRISTLICHEN WÄCHTER[16]

Schreckliche, verhexte Leiber,
Menschen-Wölf' und Drachen-Weiber!
Welch entsetzliches Getöse!
Sieh, da flammt, da zieht der Böse!
Aus dem Boden
Dampfet rings ein Höllen-Broden.

A CHRISTIAN GUARD AND CHORUS OF CHRISTIAN GUARDS

Horrible, bewitched corpses,
wolf-men and dragon-women!
What a terrible ruckus!
Look, the Evil One flames and blisters!
Out of the earth
a hellish broth boils up around us.

Strophe 12

EIN DRUIDE (2) UND CHOR DER DRUIDEN UND DES HEIDENVOLKS[17]

Die Flamme reinigt sich vom Rauch:
So reinig' unsern Glauben!
Und raubt man uns den alten Brauch:
Dein Licht, wer kann es rauben!

A DRUID AND CHORUS OF DRUIDS AND PAGAN PEOPLE

The flame purifies itself of smoke:
thus purify our faith!
And if we are robbed of our ancient rite,
who can rob us of your light!

Notes

1. There are in fact two personages named "Ein Druide": in strophes 1, 2, 5, and 7, the label refers to a tenor soloist (further: "Ein Druide [1]"), while in strophes 9 and 12 it refers to a baritone soloist (hereafter: "Ein Druide [2]").

2. Goethe has "Einer aus dem Volke" (a man from among the people) instead.

3. The word "christlicher" (Christian) occurs in Goethe only. Mendelssohn omits it because he does not use the word "Wächter" (guard) for the pagans. It is nevertheless implied.

4. This designation is from Goethe. Mendelssohn could not adopt it because of his decision to use of the word "Wächter" (guards) for the Christians exclusively, but here the guards are druids. In Mendelssohn's manuscripts this collective of protagonists remains nameless.

5. In Mendelssohn's manuscript this collective of protagonists remains nameless. Goethe has "Chor der Wächter," but in view of the participation of female voices this designation would seem inappropriate.

6. Mendelssohn omits "christlichen" (Christian); see note 4.

7. "No. 1" added editorially to match "no. 2," see note 12.

8. In *AS1* only; not present in Goethe.

9. Mendelssohn identified the instrumental introduction and its constituent parts in these terms in the orchestral score published in 1844. They do not appear in the sources of the 1832–33 version, but they are nevertheless implicit. See Mendelssohn's letter to his family, 13 February 1832 (cf. note 27 to introduction).

10. "Luftgesänge" in the seventh issue of *Goethes Neue Schriften* (Berlin: Ungar, 1800), reproduced in *AS1*, was changed to "Lustgesänge" in Goethe's later editions of the poem.

11. Goethe has only "Die Druiden" (the druids).

12. Goethe has "Weiber" (wives); Mendelssohn changed it to "Väter" (fathers), following his decision to entrust strophe 3 to a female.

13. "No. 2" supplied by Mendelssohn only (absent in all versions of Goethe's text).

14. Goethe has "Ein Wächter" (a guard). Mendelssohn could not adopt it because he reserves the use of this word for the Christians.

15. Goethe has "Ein Druide" (a druid) only. In *AS1*, the chorus is simply labeled "Chor der Männer" (men's chorus).

16. Goethe has only "Chor der christlichen Wächter" (chorus of Christian guards). Mendelssohn, in turn, has "Ein Wächter" and "Chor der Wächter" (see note 4).

17. Goethe has only "Chor der Druiden" (chorus of druids). The change in the edition is suggested by the participation of female voices and follows the revised version (op. 60) of 1843/44.

Plate 1. Felix Mendelssohn Bartholdy, *Die erste Walpurgisnacht,* 1832–33 version, autograph full score, first page (I: mm. 1–10). Biblioteka Jagiellońska, Kraków, Mus. ms. autogr. F. Mendelssohn Bartholdy 37, p. 1. Used with permission.

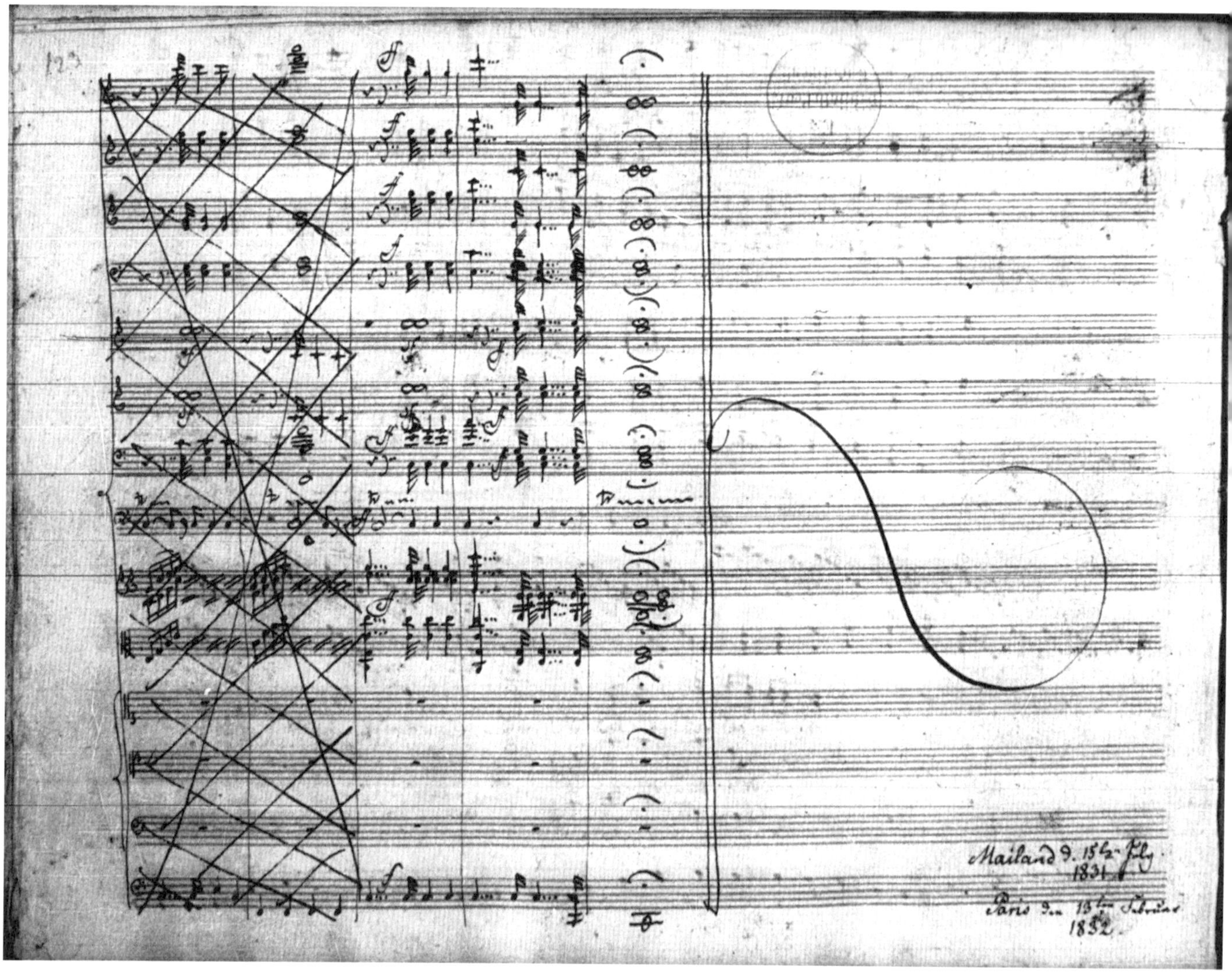

Plate 2. Felix Mendelssohn Bartholdy, *Die erste Walpurgisnacht,* 1832–33 version, autograph full score, final page (II: mm. 569–71 plus two deleted measures). Biblioteka Jagiellońska, Kraków, Mus. ms. autogr. F. Mendelssohn Bartholdy 37, p. [132]). Used with permission.

Plate 3. Felix Mendelssohn Bartholdy, *Die erste Walpurgisnacht,* 1832–33 version, autograph piano-duet arrangement of overture [1832], first page. The penciled heading in brackets, referring to "op. 60," was provided by Albert Kopfermann, director of the music division of the library from 1908 to 1914, and identifies this autograph in relation to the corresponding material in the 1843–44 version of the cantata. Staatsbibliothek zu Berlin–Preußischer Kulturbesitz, Mus. ms. autogr. F. Mendelssohn Bartholdy 49, p. [1]). Used with permission.

Plate 4. Felix Mendelssohn Bartholdy, *Die erste Walpurgisnacht,* 1832–33 version, autograph full score, II: mm. 90–104, with annotations in hand of Fanny Hensel: "2/4 Takt" and "2/4" above and beneath system at m. 92 and "2/4" and "6/8" between staves in the same measures. Biblioteka Jagiellońska, Kraków, Mus. ms. autogr. F. Mendelssohn Bartholdy 37, p. [82]. Used with permission.

Die erste Walpurgisnacht

CHARACTERS

(in order of appearance)

Ein Druide [1]—*A Druid [1]* .... tenor 1
Chor der Druiden—*Chorus of Druids* .... TTBB
Eine alte Frau—*An Old Woman* .... alto
Chor der Weiber—*Chorus of Women* .... SSAA
[Chor der Wächter des Heidenvolks]—*Chorus of Guards of the Pagan People* .... TTBB
[Chor des Heidenvolks]—*Chorus of Pagan People* .... SATB
Ein Druide [2]—*A Druid [2]* .... baritone
Ein [christlicher] Wächter—*A Christian Guard* .... tenor 2
Chor der [christlichen] Wächter—*Chorus of Christian Guards* .... TTBB
Chor der Druiden [und des Heidenvolks]—*Chorus of Druids and Pagan People* .... SATB

INSTRUMENTS

Flute (Fl.) 1, 2
Oboe (Ob.) 1, 2
Clarinet (Cl.) 1, 2 in A/B♭/C
Bassoon (Bn.) 1, 2

Horn (Hn.) 1, 2 in C/D/E
Trumpet (Tpt) 1, 2 in C/D/E
Trombone (Trb.) 1, 2, 3

Timpani (Timp.)

Violin (Vn.) 1, 2
Viola (Va.)
Violoncello (Vc.)
Contrabass (Cb.)

[No. 1:] Einleitung

[Overture: Das schlechte Wetter]

6
Fl. 1, 2
f
sf
Ob. 1, 2
sf
Cl. 1, 2
in C
sf
a 2
Bn. 1, 2
a 2
f
Hn. 1, 2
in C
sf
Tpt. 1, 2
in D
f
Trb. 1, 2
Trb. 3
Timp.
Vn. 1
sf
Vn. 2
sf
Va.
Vc.
Cb.

10
sf
sf
a 2
f
sf
sf

14
Ob. 1, 2
Cl. 1, 2
in C
Bn. 1, 2
Hn. 1, 2
in C
Tpt. 1, 2
in D
Vn. 1
Vn. 2
Va.
Vc.
Cb.
a 2
f
18
cresc.

22
a 2
tr
f
fsf
sf

26
Fl. 1, 2
Ob. 1, 2
Cl. 1, 2
in C
Bn. 1
Bn. 2
Hn. 1, 2
in C
Tpt. 1, 2
in D
Trb. 1, 2
Trb. 3
Timp.
Vn. 1
Vn. 2
Va.
Vc.
Cb.
ff
ff
ff
ff
sempre f
sempre f

30
ff
tr
ff

34
Fl. 1, 2
Ob. 1, 2
Cl. 1, 2
in C
Bn. 1, 2
Hn. 1, 2
in C
Tpt. 1, 2
in D
Trb. 1, 2
Trb. 3
tr
Timp.
Vn. 1
sf
Vn. 2
sf
Va.
Vc.
Cb.

42
Fl. 1, 2
Ob. 1, 2
Cl. 1, 2
in C
Bn. 1, 2
Hn. 1, 2
in C
Tpt. 1, 2
in D
Trb. 1, 2
Trb. 3
Timp.
Vn. 1
Vn. 2
Va.
Vc.
Cb.

*See Text-Genetic Remarks (I: mm. 48–49) and Appendix I.1.

50
Fl. 1, 2
Ob. 1, 2
Cl. 1, 2
in C
Bn. 1, 2
Hn. 1, 2
in C
Tpt. 1, 2
in D
f
a 2
Trb. 1, 2
Trb. 3
Timp.
Vn. 1
Vn. 2
Va.
Vc.
Cb.

*See Text-Genetic Remarks (I: mm. 57–64).

58
Fl. 1, 2
Ob. 1, 2
Cl. 1, 2 in C
Bn. 1, 2
Hn. 1, 2 in C
Tpt. 1, 2 in D
Trb. 1, 2
Trb. 3
Timp.
Vn. 1
Vn. 2
Va.
Vc.
Cb.

*See Text-Genetic Remarks (I: mm. 64–65) and Appendix I.2.

66
Fl. 1, 2
Ob. 1, 2
Cl. 1, 2
in C
Bn. 1, 2
Vn. 1
Vn. 2
Va.
Vc.
Cb.
sf
simile
cresc.
70
p
[dim.]
dim.

74
sf
cresc.
sf
cresc.
sf
cresc.
sf
cresc.
cresc.
78
ritardando
1
p
p
p
ritardando
sfz
dim.
sf
sf
[dim.]
sf
f
sf
fsf
sf
fsf
sf

*See Text-Genetic Remarks (I: mm. 82–83) and Appendix I.3.

tr
cresc.
cresc.

90
Fl. 1, 2
Ob. 1, 2
Cl. 1, 2
in C
Bn. 1, 2
Hn. 1, 2
in C
a 2
f
Tpt. 1, 2
in D
Trb. 1, 2
cresc.
ff
Trb. 3
cresc.
ff
Timp.
ff
Vn. 1
ff
Vn. 2
ff
Va.
[cresc.]
ff
Vc.
[cresc.]
ff
Cb.
cresc.
ff

94
a 2
p
dim.
a 2
f
p
f
p
tr
f
p
dim.
dim.
dim.
dim.
dim.

98
Fl. 1, 2
Ob. 1, 2
Cl. 1, 2
in C
a 2
p
Bn. 1, 2
a 2
p
Tpt. 1, 2
in D
Trb. 1, 2
Trb. 3
Timp.
Vn. 1
p
agitato
Vn. 2
p
Va.
p
Vc.
pizz.
arco
p
Cb.
pizz.

102
a 2
p
a 2
p
p
p
pizz.

106
Fl. 1, 2
Ob. 1, 2
Cl. 1, 2
in C
Bn. 1, 2
Hn. 1, 2
in C
a 2
p
Tpt. 1, 2
in D
Trb. 1, 2
p
Trb. 3
p
Timp.
p
Vn. 1
p
Vn. 2
Va.
Vc.
Cb.

110
cresc.
cresc.
p
(>)
p
p
p
p

114
Fl. 1, 2
più f
Ob. 1, 2
più f
Cl. 1, 2 in C
Bn. 1, 2
cresc.
Hn. 1, 2 in C
cresc.
Tpt. 1, 2 in D
a 2
p
Trb. 1, 2
cresc.
cresc.
Trb. 3
cresc.
cresc.
Timp.
Vn. 1
cresc.
Vn. 2
cresc.
Va.
p
Vc.
arco
Cb.
arco

118
cresc. sempre
cresc.
[cresc.]
cresc.
cresc.
cresc.
cresc.
cresc.
cresc.

122
Fl. 1, 2
Ob. 1, 2
Cl. 1, 2 in C
Bn. 1, 2
Hn. 1, 2 in C
Tpt. 1, 2 in D
Trb. 1, 2
Trb. 3
Timp.
Vn. 1
Vn. 2
Va.
Vc.
Cb.
f cresc. al
a 2
cresc.
cresc. al

B
126
ff
a 2
a 2
a 2
tr

131
Fl. 1, 2
Ob. 1, 2
Cl. 1, 2 in C
Bn. 1, 2
Hn. 1, 2 in C
Tpt. 1, 2 in D
a 2
Trb. 1, 2
a 2
Trb. 3
sf
(tr)
Timp.
Vn. 1
Vn. 2
Va.
Vc.
Cb.

136
a 2
tr

141
Fl. 1, 2
Ob. 1, 2
Cl. 1, 2
in C
Bn. 1, 2
Hn. 1, 2
in C
Tpt. 1, 2
in D
Trb. 1, 2
Trb. 3
Timp.
Vn. 1
Vn. 2
Va.
Vc.
Cb.

146
a 2
f
f
a 2
f
f
f
151

156
Fl. 1, 2
Ob. 1, 2
Cl. 1, 2
in C
Bn. 1, 2
Hn. 1, 2
in C
Vn. 1
Vn. 2
Va.
Vc.
Cb.
f
f
161
[a 2]
a 2
sf
sf

166
a 2
sf
f
171
più f

176
Fl. 1, 2
Ob. 1, 2
Cl. 1, 2 in C
Bn. 1, 2
Hn. 1, 2 in C
Tpt. 1, 2 in D
Trb. 1, 2
Trb. 3
Timp.
Vn. 1
Vn. 2
Va.
Vc.
Cb.
ff
tr

*See Text-Genetic Remarks (I: m. 183).

186
Fl. 1, 2
Bn. 1, 2
Trb. 3
Va.
Vc.
Cb.
psf
sf
p
191
Ob. 1, 2
Cl. 1, 2
in C
Vn. 1
Vn. 2
a 2
p cresc.

196
cresc.
[cresc.]
[cresc.]
cresc.
p
tr
p
cresc.
cresc. al
cresc.
cresc. al
cresc.
cresc. al
cresc. al
cresc. al

*See Text-Genetic Remarks (I: mm. 201–2) and Appendix I.4.

206
dim. sempre
dim. sempre
dim.
dim.
dim.
dim.
dim.

211
Fl. 1, 2
Ob. 1, 2
Cl. 1, 2
in C
Bn. 1, 2
Hn. 1, 2
in C
Tpt. 1, 2
in D
Timp.
Vn. 1
Vn. 2
Va.
Vc.
Cb.
pp
p
tr

216
1
pp
cresc.
p
cresc.
pp
cresc.
p
cresc.
p [cresc.]
(tr)
221
p [cresc.]
f
p cresc.
f
f
f
p
cresc.
f
mf
[cresc.]
f
mf

*See Text-Genetic Remarks (I: mm. 228–29) and Appendix I.5.

231
f
sf
a 2
tr
p

236
Fl. 1, 2
Ob. 1, 2
Cl. 1, 2 in C
Bn. 1, 2
a 2
Hn. 1, 2 in C
Tpt. 1, 2 in D
Trb. 1, 2
Trb. 3
Timp.
f
Vn. 1
sf
Vn. 2
sf
Va.
Vc.
Cb.
sf
sf

*See Text-Genetic Remarks (I: mm. 247–48) and Appendix I.6.

251
Fl. 1, 2
Ob. 1, 2
Cl. 1, 2 in C
Bn. 1, 2
Timp.
Vn. 1
Vn. 2
Va.
Vc.
Cb.
dim.
[dim.]
sul G
256
Fl. 1, 2
Cl. 1, 2 in C
Bn. 1, 2
Hn. 1, 2 in C
Vn. 1
Vn. 2
Va.
Vc.
Cb.
cresc.
[cresc.]
a 2

261
E
f cresc. al
ff
sf
cresc.
a 2
tr
cresc. al

266
Fl. 1, 2
Ob. 1, 2
Cl. 1, 2 in C
Bn. 1, 2
Hn. 1, 2 in C
Tpt. 1, 2 in D
Trb. 1, 2
Trb. 3
tr
Timp.
Vn. 1
Vn. 2
Va.
Vc.
Cb.

272
f
f

278
Fl. 1
Fl. 2
Ob. 1
Ob. 2
Cl. 1
in C
Cl. 2
in C
Bn. 1
Bn. 2
Hn. 1, 2
in C
Tpt. 1, 2
in D
Trb. 1, 2
Trb. 3
Timp.
Vn. 1
Vn. 2
Va.
Vc.
Cb.
f
ff
tr

283
f
tr

288
Fl. 1, 2
Ob. 1, 2
Cl. 1, 2
in C
Bn. 1, 2
Hn. 1, 2
in C
Tpt. 1, 2
in D
Trb. 1, 2
Trb. 3
tr
Timp.
Vn. 1
Vn. 2
Va.
Vc.
Cb.

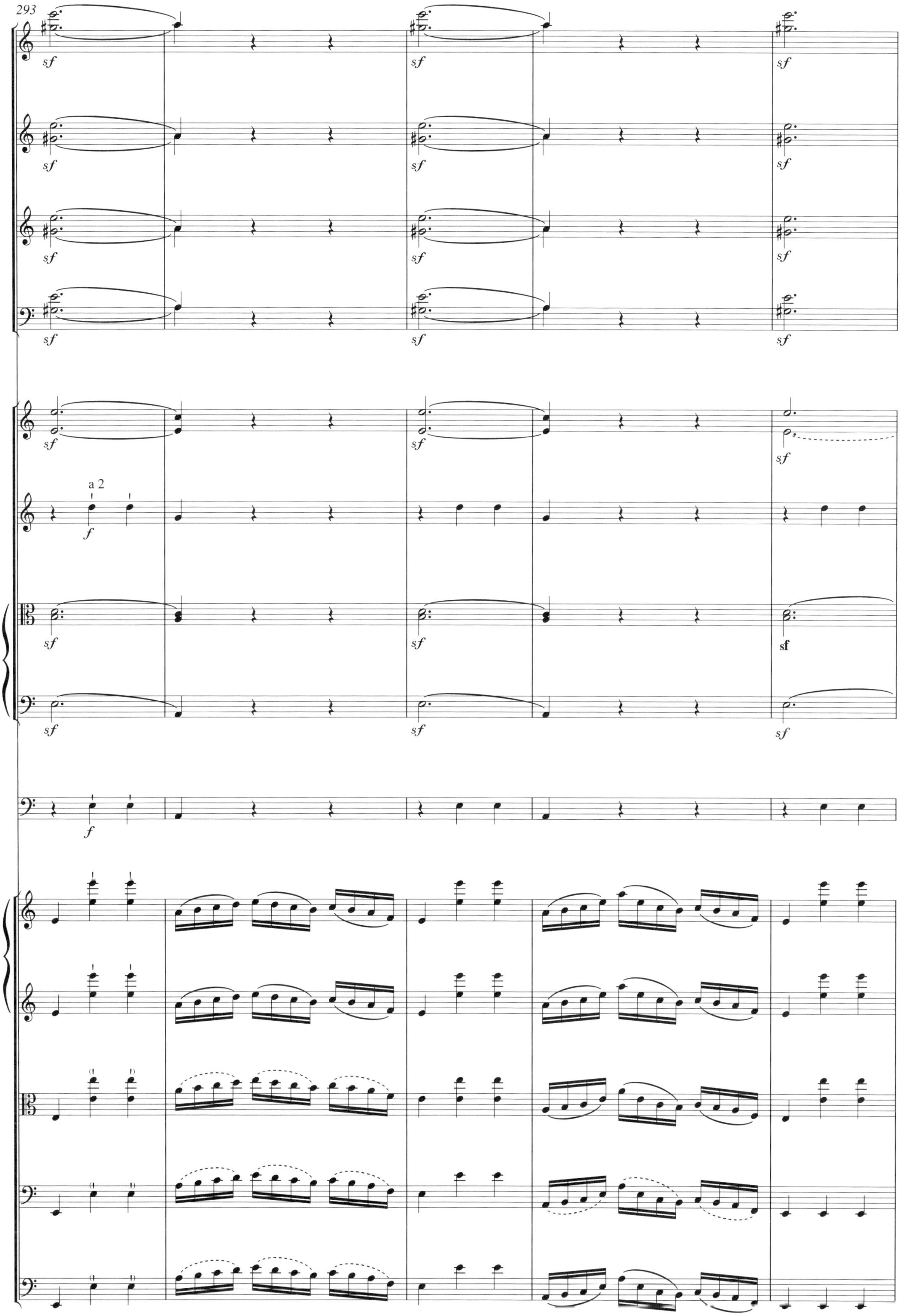
293
sf
a 2
f

298
Fl. 1
Fl. 2
Ob. 1, 2
Cl. 1, 2
in C
Bn. 1, 2
Hn. 1, 2
in C
Tpt. 1, 2
in D
Trb. 1, 2
Trb. 3
Timp.
Vn. 1
Vn. 2
Va.
Vc.
Cb.
ff
a 2
f

F
302
ff
1
p
in A
in E
dim.

307
Fl. 1
Fl. 2
p
Bn. 1, 2
p
Hn. 1, 2
in C
1
p
Vn. 1
p
dim.
Vn. 2
p
dim.
divisi
Va.
pp
Vc.
p
[dim.]
Cb.
p
[dim.]
312
pp
Fl. 1, 2
Bn. 1, 2
pp
Hn. 1, 2
in C
Vn. 1
dim.
Vn. 2
dim.
Va.
Vc.
p
Cb.

319
in A
1
tr
pizz.
325
pizz.
divisi
pizz.
arco

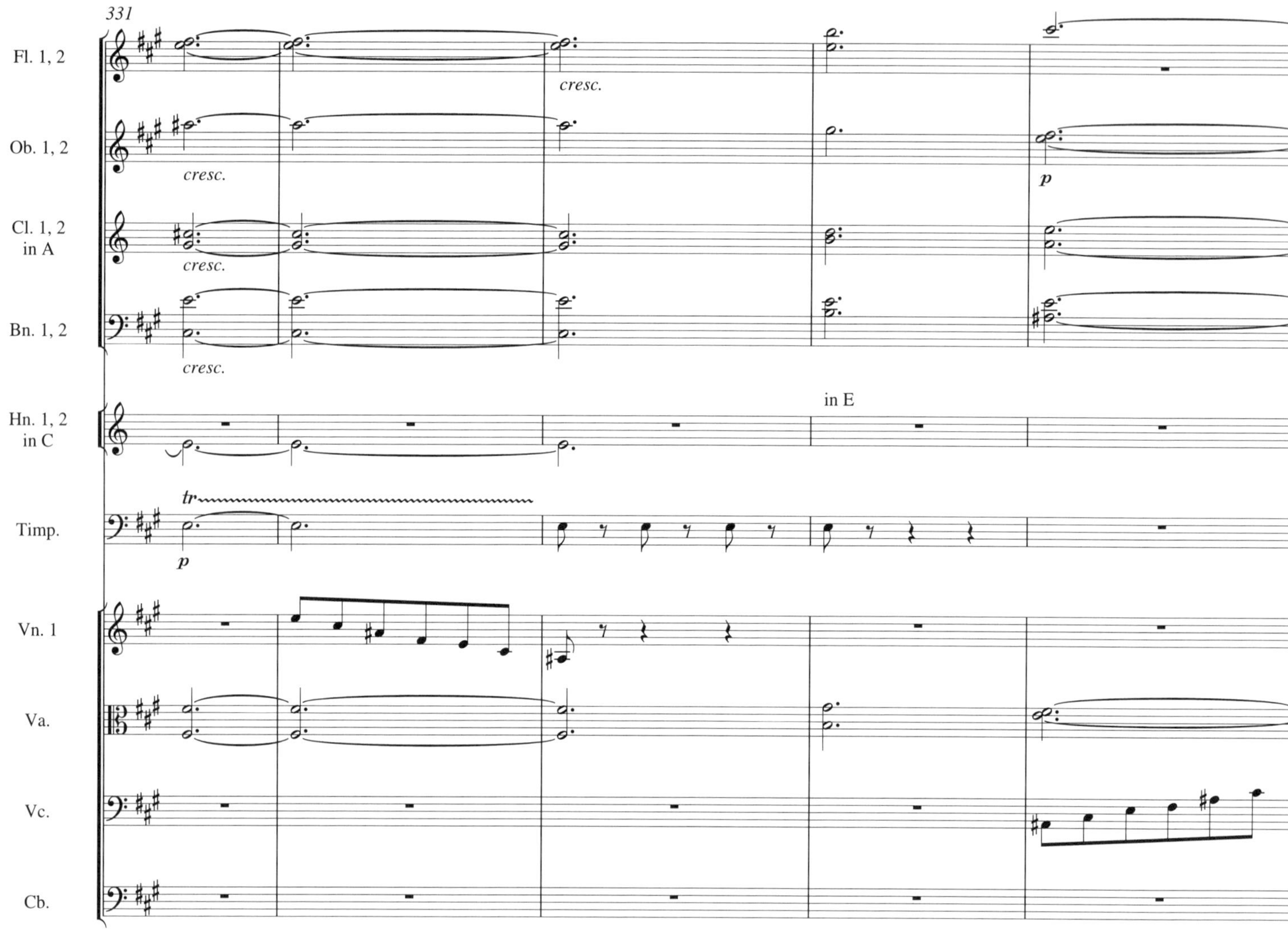
331
Fl. 1, 2
Ob. 1, 2
Cl. 1, 2
in A
Bn. 1, 2
Hn. 1, 2
in C
Timp.
Vn. 1
Va.
Vc.
Cb.
cresc.
cresc.
cresc.
cresc.
p
in E
tr
p

336
Fl. 1, 2
Ob. 1, 2
Cl. 1, 2
in A
Bn. 1, 2
Vn. 1
Va.
Vc.
Cb.
p
f
pizz.

[Der Übergang zum Frühling]

347
Fl. 1, 2
Ob. 1, 2
Cl. 1, 2 in A
Bn. 1, 2
Hn. 1, 2 in E
in E
Tpt. 1, 2 in E
Timp.
Vn. 1
[arco]
Vn. 2
Va.
Vc.
Cb.
arco

352
1
p
f
sf
in E
pp
tr
divisi

358
Fl. 1, 2
Ob. 1, 2
p
Cl. 1, 2
in A
p
sf
Bn. 1, 2
Hn. 1, 2
in E
dolce
Tpt. 1, 2
in E
p
Timp.
tr
pp
Vn. 1
p
Vn. 2
Va.
p
Vc.
Cb.

364

371
Fl. 1, 2
Ob. 1, 2
Cl. 1, 2 in A
p
[cresc.]
cresc.
Bn. 1, 2
cresc.
[cresc.]
Hn. 1, 2 in E
p
cresc.
cresc.
Tpt. 1, 2 in E
Timp.
Vn. 1
cresc.
Vn. 2
cresc.
Va.
[cresc.]
Vc.
cresc.
Cb.
cresc.

378
G
p
cresc.
[cresc.]
tr
pp
mf
[divisi]
[unisono]
mf

383
Fl. 1
Fl. 2
Ob. 1, 2
Cl. 1, 2
in A
Bn. 1, 2
Hn. 1, 2
in E
Tpt. 1, 2
in E
Timp.
Vn. 1
Vn. 2
Va.
Vc.
Cb.
[cresc.]
cresc.
tr
p
cresc. al
[cresc. al]

388
dim.
cresc.
f
dim.
[dim.]
in D
mf
(tr)
dim.
divisi
[dim.]

393
Fl. 1, 2
Ob. 1, 2
Cl. 1, 2 in A
Bn. 1, 2
Hn. 1, 2 in D
Tpt. 1, 2 in E
Timp.
Vn. 1
Vn. 2
Va.
Vc.
Cb.
p
pp
dim.
[divisi]
[unisono]
[dim.]

399
[Strophe 1]
Es lacht der Mai! Der Wald ist frei von Eis und Reif- ge-
Now May a- gain breaks win- ter's chain, the bud and bloom are
405
-hän- ge.
spring- ing;
Es lacht der Mai! Der Wald ist
Now May a- gain breaks win- ter's
[unisono]

411
Fl. 1, 2
Cl. 1, 2 in A
Bn. 1, 2
Druide [1]
frei von Eis und Reif- ge- hän- ge. Der Schnee ist fort; am grü- nen
chain, the bud and bloom are spring- ing; no snow is seen; the vales are
Vn. 1
Vn. 2
Va.
Vc.
Cb.
p
417
Fl. 1, 2
Cl. 1, 2 in A
Bn. 1, 2
Hn. 1, 2 in D
Druide [1]
Ort er- schal- len Luft- ge- sän- ge.
green, the wood- land choirs are sing- ing.
Vn. 1
Vn. 2
Va.
divisi
[unisono]
Vc.
Cb.
mf

423
Der Schnee ist fort; am grü- nen Ort er- schal- len Luft- ge-
No snow is seen; the vales are green, the wood-land choirs are
divisi
[unisono]
429
-sän- ge, am grü- nen, grü- nen Ort er- schal- len Luft- ge- sän-
sing- ing, the vales, vales are green, the wood-land choirs are sing-

435
Fl. 1, 2
Cl. 1, 2 in A
Bn. 1, 2
Hn. 1, 2 in D
Druide [1]
-ge. Der Schnee, der Schnee ist fort; am grü- nen Ort er- schal- len
-ing. No snow, no snow is seen; the vales are green, the wood- land
Vn. 1
Vn. 2
Va.
Vc.
Cb.
cresc.
[cresc.]
pizz.
441
Luft- ge- sän- ge. Es lacht der
choirs are sing- ing. Now May a-
arco

447
dim.
dolce
Mai!
-gain
Der Wald ist frei!
breaks win- - ter's chain!
dim.
pp
453
pizz.
Ein rei- ner Schnee liegt auf der Höh'; doch ei- len wir nach
Yon moun-tain height is win- t'ry white; up- on it we will

460
Fl. 1, 2
Cl. 1, 2 in A
Bn. 1, 2
Druide [1]
pp
o- ben, be- gehn den al- ten heil'- gen
gath- er. Be- gin the an- cient ho- ly
Vn. 1
Vn. 2
Va.
Vc.
Cb.
arco
pp
466
accelerando
cresc.
[cresc.]
p
Brauch, be- gehn den al- ten heil'- gen Brauch,
rite; be- gin the an- cient ho- ly rite;
poco a poco crescendo al

*See Text-Genetic Remarks (I: mm. 473–74).

480
[Strophe 2]
Allegro con fuoco
Fl. 1, 2
Ob. 1, 2
Cl. 1, 2 in A
Bn. 1, 2
Hn. 1, 2 in D
Druide [1]
Die Flam- me lod- re durch den Rauch!
In sac- ri- fice the flame shall rise;
Vn. 1
Vn. 2
Va.
Vc.
Cb.
cresc.
[cresc.]

486
Die Flam- me lod- re
in sac- ri- fice the

491
Druide [1]
durch den __ Rauch! Be- geht den al- ten heil'- gen __ Brauch,
flame shall __ rise; be- gin the an- cient ho- ly ____ rite,
Vn. 1
Vn. 2
Va.
Vc.
Cb.

497
Druide [1]
All- va- ter dort zu lo- ben, All- va- ter dort zu lo-
praise our Al- might- y Fa- ther, praise our Al- might- y Fa-
Vn. 1
Vn. 2
Va.
Vc.
Cb.

*See Text-Genetic Remarks (I: mm. 507–8) and Appendix I.6.

515
Fl. 1, 2
Ob. 1, 2
Cl. 1, 2 in A
Bn. 1, 2
Hn. 1, 2 in D
Druide [1]
ben.
er.
CHOR DER DRUIDEN
T1
T2
B1
B2
cresc.
[cresc.]
Die Flam- me lod- - re, lod-
In sac- ri- fice the flame,
Vn. 1
Vn. 2
Va.
Vc.
Cb.
pizz.

521
re durch den Rauch! Be- geht den al- ten heil'- gen Brauch, All-
the flame shall rise! Be- gin the an- cient ho- ly rite; All- praise
arco

527
Fl. 1, 2
Ob. 1, 2
Cl. 1, 2 in A
Bn. 1, 2
Hn. 1, 2 in D
Druide [1]
CHOR DER DRUIDEN
T1
T2
B1
B2
-va- ter dort zu lo- ben, All- va- ter dort zu
our Al- might- y Fa- ther, praise our Al- might- y
Vn. 1
Vn. 2
Va.
Vc.
Cb.
f
sf

*See Text-Genetic Remarks (I: mm. 533–34).

539
Fl. 1, 2
Ob. 1, 2
Cl. 1, 2 in A
Bn. 1, 2
Hn. 1, 2 in D
Druide [1]
-auf! Hin- auf nach o- ben!
-way! A- way! A- way!
CHOR DER DRUIDEN
T1
-auf! Hin- auf nach o- ben! Die Flam- me lod- re
-way! A- way! A- way! In sac- ri- fice the
T2
-auf! Hin- auf nach o- ben! Die Flam- me
-way! A- way! A- way! the flame shall
B1
-auf! Hin- auf nach o- ben! Die Flam- me lod- - re
-way! A- way! A- way! In sac- ri- fice the
B2
-auf! Hin- auf nach o- ben! Die Flam- me
-way! A- way! A- way! the flame shall
Vn. 1
Vn. 2
Va.
Vc.
Cb.

545
1
p
cresc.
[cresc.]
Be- geht den heil'- gen Brauch,
Be- gin the ho- ly rite,
durch den Rauch! Be- geht den al- ten heil'- gen Brauch,
flame shall rise! Be- gin the an- cient ho- ly rite,
lod- re Be- geht den heil'- gen Brauch,
rise, shall rise! Be- gin the ho- ly rite,
f
durch den Rauch! Be- geht den al- - ten heil'- gen Brauch, be-
flame shall rise! Be- gin the an- - cient ho- ly rite, be-
f
lod- re Be- geht den heil'- gen Brauch, be-
rise, shall rise! Be- gin the ho- ly rite, be-
cresc.
[cresc.]
[cresc.]
cresc.
f
cresc.
f

551
Fl. 1, 2
Ob. 1, 2
a 2
Cl. 1, 2 in A
Bn. 1, 2
a 2
Hn. 1, 2 in D
Druide [1]
be- geht den heil'- gen Brauch, be- geht den al- ten
be- gin the ho- ly rite; be- gin the an- cient
CHOR DER DRUIDEN
T1
be- geht den heil'- gen Brauch, be- geht den al- ten
be- gin the ho- ly rite; be- gin the an- cient
T2
be- geht den heil'- gen Brauch, be- geht den al- ten
be- gin the ho- ly rite; be- gin the an- cient
B1
-geht den al- ten heil'- gen Brauch, be- geht den al- ten
-gin the an- cient ho- ly rite; be- gin the an- cient
B2
-geht den al- ten heil'- gen Brauch, be- geht den al- ten
-gin the an- cient ho- ly rite; be- gin the an- cient
Vn. 1
Vn. 2
Va.
Vc.
Cb.

557
p
cresc.
molto cresc.
mf
heil'- gen Brauch, die Flam- me lod- - re durch den Rauch!
ho- ly rite; in sac- ri- fice the flame shall rise!
lod- re durch den Rauch!
fice the flame shall rise!
cresc. molto
sf

563
Fl. 1, 2
Ob. 1, 2
Cl. 1, 2 in A
Bn. 1, 2
Hn. 1, 2 in D
Druide [1]
Hin- auf! Hin- auf nach o- - ben. Hin-
A- way! A- way! A- way! A- way! A-
CHOR DER DRUIDEN
T1
T2
B1
Hin- auf! Hin- auf nach o- - ben.
A- way! A- way! A- way! A- way!
B2
Hin- auf nach o- - ben.
A- way! A- way! A- way!
Vn. 1
Vn. 2
Va.
Vc.
Cb.
cresc.

569
-auf! Hin- auf! Hin- auf! Hin-
-way! A- way! A- way! A-
-auf! Hin- auf! Hin- auf! Hin-
-way! A- way! A- way! A-
-auf! Hin- auf! Hin- auf! Hin-
-way! A- way! A- way! A-
Hin- auf! Hin- auf! Hin- auf! Hin-
A- way! A- way! A- way! A-
Hin- auf! Hin- auf! Hin- auf! Hin-
A- way! A- way! A- way! A-

575
Fl. 1, 2
Ob. 1, 2
Cl. 1, 2 in A
Bn. 1, 2
Hn. 1, 2 in D
Druide [1]
-auf nach o- - ben!
-way! A- way! A- way!
CHOR DER DRUIDEN
T1
-auf nach o- - ben!
-way! A- way! A- way!
T2
-auf nach o- - ben!
-way! A- way! A- way!
B1
-auf nach o- - ben!
-way! A- way! A- way!
B2
-auf nach o- - ben!
-way! A- way! A- way!
Vn. 1
Vn. 2
Va.
Vc.
Cb.
ff
sf

581
sf
ff
sf
ff
ff
ff
ff
sf
sf
sf
sf
sf
sf
sf
sf
sf
sf
sf
sf
sf
sf
sf

[Strophe 3]
Allegretto
586
Fl. 1, 2
Ob. 1, 2
Cl. 1, 2 in A
Bn. 1, 2
[in E]
Hn. 1, 2 in D
Allegretto
Alte Frau
p
Könnt ihr so ver- we- gen han- deln? Wollt ihr denn zum
Know ye not a deed so dar- ing, dooms us all to
Allegretto
Vn. 1
Vn. 2
Va.
Vc.
Cb.
592
sempre mezza
To- de wan- deln? Ken- net ihr nicht die Ge- set- ze uns- rer har- ten Ü- ber- win- der?
die de- spair- ing? Know ye not it is for- bid- den by the e- dicts of our foe- men?

598
Rings ge- stellt sind ih- re Net- ze auf die Hei- den, auf die Sün- der. Ach, sie schlach- ten
Know ye, spies and snares are hid- den for the sin- ners call'd "the Hea- then"? On their ram- parts
604
auf dem Wal- le uns- re Vä- ter, uns- re Kin-
they will slaugh- ter moth- er, fa- ther, son, and daugh-

610
Alte Frau
-der. Ach, sie schlach-ten auf dem Wal- le uns- re Kin- der. Ach, sie schlach- ten schon uns- re
-ter! On their ram- parts they will slaugh- ter moth- er, fa- ther, son, and daugh- ter! moth- er,
sf
Vn. 1
Vn. 2
Va.
Vc.
Cb.

616
Alte Frau
Vä- ter, uns- re Kin- der! Und wir al- -
fa- ther, son, and daugh- ter! If de- tect- -
p
Vn. 1
Vn. 2
Va.
Vc.
Cb.
sf
pp

623
cresc.
sf
p
-le, und wir al- le, al- le, al- le na- hen uns ge-
-ed, naught but death can be ex- pect- ed, naught but death can
cresc.
pp
pp
pp
cresc.
pp
cresc.
pp
cresc.
pp
630
-wis- sem Fal- le, na- hen uns ge- wis- sem Fal- -
be ex- pect- ed, naught but death can be ex- pect- -
tr
tr
tr
tr
tr

H
637
[Strophe 4]
Alte Frau
-le.
-ed.
CHOR DER WEIBER
S
A
Auf des La- gers ho- hem Wal- le schlach-ten sie schon uns- re Kin-
On their ram-parts they will slaugh- ter moth- er, fa- ther, son, and daugh-
Vn. 1
Vn. 2
Va.
Vc.
Cb.
642
Und wir
If de-
-der. Ach, die stren- gen Ü- ber- win- der! Und wir
-ter! They op- press us, They dis- tress us! If de-

648
cresc. al
f
al- le na- hen uns ge- wis- sem Fal-
-tect- ed, naught but death can be ex- pect-
al- le na- hen uns ge- wis- sem Fal- le.
-tect- ed, naught but death can be ex- pect- ed.
653
le.
ed.
sf
Auf des La- gers ho- hem Wal- le schlach-ten sie schon uns- re
On their ram-parts they will slaugh- ter moth- er, fa- ther, son, and

658
CHOR DER WEIBER
S
A
Kin- der! Ach, die stren- gen Ü- ber-
daugh- ter, moth- er, fa- ther, son, and
Vn. 1
Vn. 2
Va.
Vc.
Cb.
663
Druide [1]
Wer
The
-win- der! Ach, die stren- gen, ach, die stren- gen Ü- ber- win-
daugh- ter! If de- tect- ed, naught but death can be ex- pect-

668
[Strophe 5]
Allegro vivace
Allegro vivace
Op- fer heut' zu brin- gen scheut, ver- dient erst
man who flies our sac- ri- fice de- serves the
-der!
-ed!
-der!
-ed!
Allegro vivace
f non legato
p cresc.
f
p cresc.
f
f
p cresc.
f
p cresc.

673
Fl. 1, 2
con fuoco
Ob. 1, 2
[con fuoco]
Cl. 1, 2 in A
[con fuoco]
Bn. 1, 2
[con fuoco]
Hn. 1, 2 in E
in E
con fuoco
Tpt. 1, 2 in E
con fuoco
Druide [1]
sei- ne Ban- de. Der Wald ist frei! Der Wald ist
ty- rant's teth- er. The woods are free! The woods are
Vn. 1
Vn. 2
Va.
mf
cresc.
Vc.
Cb.

679
frei! Das Holz her- bei, und schich- tet es zum
free! Dis-branch the tree, and pile the stems to-

*See Text-Genetic Remarks (I: mm. 689–90) and Appendix I.8.

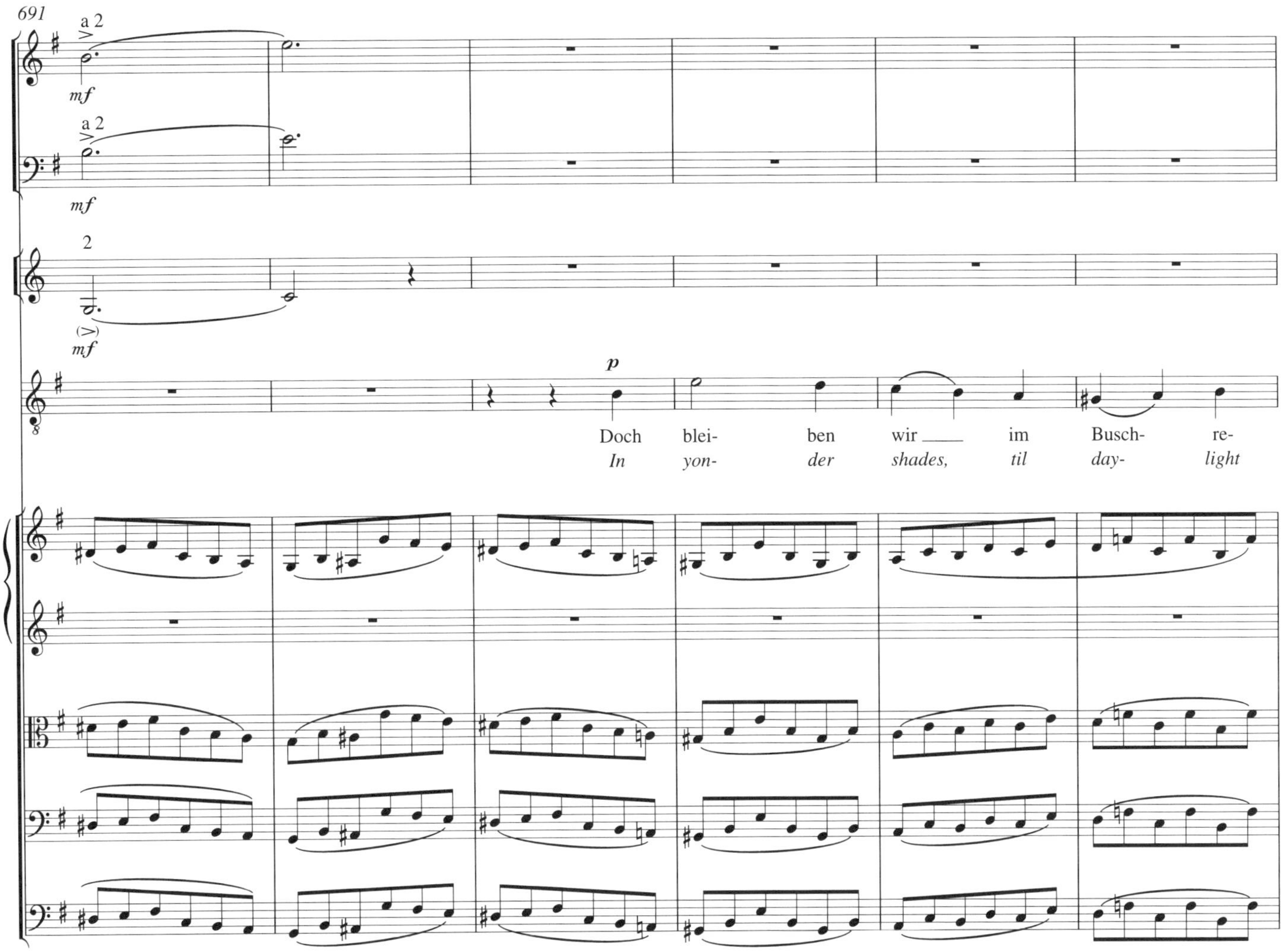
691
a 2
mf
a 2
mf
2
(>)
mf
p
Doch blei- ben wir im Busch- re-
In yon- der shades, til day- light

697
a 2
p
a 2
p
-vier am Ta- ge noch im Stil- len,
fades, we shall not be de- tect- ed;
pp

*See Text-Genetic Remarks (I: mm. 702–3) and Appendix I.9.

715
p
cresc.
cresc. al
-len. Dann a- ber lasst mit fri- schem Mut uns un- sre
-ed. Con- quer with cour- age sla- vish fear; show du- ty's

*See Text-Genetic Remarks (I: mm. 723–24) and Appendix I.10.

726
f
lasst, dann a- ber lasst mit fri- schem Mut
cour- age, con- quer with cour- age sla- vish fear;

731
Fl. 1, 2
Ob. 1, 2
Cl. 1, 2
in A
Bn. 1, 2
Hn. 1, 2
in E
Tpt. 1, 2
in E
Druide [1]
uns un- sre Pflicht er- fül- len. Dann a- ber
show du- ty's claim re- spect- ed! Con- quer with
Vn. 1
Vn. 2
Va.
Vc.
Cb.

736
p
cresc.
f
cresc.
lasst,
cour-
-
age
f
dann
a-
ber
sla-
vish
[cresc.]

[Strophe 6]
Allegro leggiero
741
Recit.
Tempo 1mo
marcato
Hn. 1, 2 in E
Druide [1]
forte assai
lasst, dann a- ber lasst mit fri-schem Mut uns un-sre Pflicht er- fül- len.
fear; con-quer with cour-age sla-vish fear; show du-ty's claim re- spect- ed!
Vn. 1
Vn. 2
Va.
Vc.
Cb.
pizz.
746
Fl. 1, 2
Cl. 1, 2 in A
Bn. 1, 2
Hn. 1, 2 in E
Tpt. 1, 2 in E
a 2
dim.
marcato

752
pp
p
1
pp
p
p
sempre pizz.
p
sempre pizz.
p
sempre pizz.
p
sempre pizz.
pp
[sempre pizz.]
pp

758
Fl. 1, 2
Ob. 1, 2
Cl. 1, 2 in A
Bn. 1, 2
Hn. 1, 2 in E
Tpt. 1, 2 in E
[CHOR DER WÄCHTER DES HEIDENVOLKS]
T1
Ver-teilt euch, wack- re Män-ner, hier Ver- teilt euch
Dis-perse, dis- perse, ye gal- lant men! Dis- perse, ye
T2
Ver-teilt euch hier Ver- teilt euch
Dis-perse, dis- perse, dis- perse, ye
B1
Ver-teilt euch, wack- re Män-ner, hier Ver- teilt euch
Dis-perse, dis- perse, ye gal- lant men! Dis- perse, ye
B2
Ver-teilt euch, wack- re Män- ner,
Dis-perse, dis- perse, ye gal- lant
Vn. 1
Vn. 2
Va.
Vc.
Cb.

763
pp
a 2
p
p
p
pp
hier, Ver- teilt euch, wack- re Män- ner, hier durch die- ses gan- ze Wald- re- vier und
men! Dis- perse, dis- perse, ye gal- lant men! Se- cure the pass- es round the glen: In
pp
hier, Ver- teilt euch, wack- re Män- ner, hier durch die- ses gan- ze Wald- re- vier und
men! Dis- perse, dis- perse, ye gal- lant men! Se- cure the pass- es round the glen: In
pp
hier, Ver- teilt euch, wack- re Män- ner, hier durch die- ses gan- ze Wald- re- vier und
men! Dis- perse, dis- perse, ye gal- lant men! Se- cure the pass- es round the glen: In
pp
hier, Ver- teilt euch, wack- re Män- ner, hier durch die- ses gan- ze Wald- re- vier und
men! Dis- perse, dis- perse, ye gal- lant men! Se- cure the pass- es round the glen: In

768
Fl. 1, 2
Ob. 1, 2
Cl. 1, 2 in A
Bn. 1, 2
Hn. 1, 2 in E
Tpt. 1, 2 in E
[CHOR DER WÄCHTER DES HEIDENVOLKS]
T1
T2
B1
B2
wa- chet hier im Stil- len, wenn sie die Pflicht er-
si- lence there pro- tect them, whose du- ties here di-
Vn. 1
Vn. 2
Va.
Vc.
Cb.
p
cresc.
pp

774
-fül- len, und wa- chet hier im Stil- len, wenn sie die Pflicht er- fül- len, im
-rect them. In si- lence there pro- tect them, whose du- ties here di- rect them. In
-fül- len, und wa- chet hier im Stil- len, wenn sie die Pflicht er- fül- len, im
-rect them. In si- lence there pro- tect them, whose du- ties here di- rect them. In
-fül- len, wenn sie die Pflicht er- fül- len, im
-rect them, whose du- ties here di- rect them. In
-ful- len, wenn sie die Pflicht er- fül- len, im
-rect them, whose du- ties here di- rect them. In

780
Fl. 1, 2
Ob. 1, 2
Cl. 1, 2 in A
Bn. 1, 2
Hn. 1, 2 in E
Tpt. 1, 2 in E
[CHOR DER WÄCHTER DES HEIDENVOLKS]
T1
Stil- len, im Stil- len, ver- teilt euch, wack- re
si- lence, in si- lence, Dis- perse, dis- perse, ye
T2
Stil- len, im Stil- len, ver-
si- lence, in si- lence, dis-
B1
Stil- len, im Stil- len, ver- teilt euch, wack- re Män- ner, hier, ver- teilt euch,
si- lence, in si- lence, Dis- perse, dis- perse, ye gal- lant men! Dis- perse, dis-
B2
Stil- len, im Stil- len,
si- lence, in si- lence,
Vn. 1
Vn. 2
Va.
Vc.
Cb.
p
pp
cresc.

785
a 2
Män- ner, hier im Stil- len, ver- teilt euch, wack- re Män- ner, hier durch
gal- lant men! In si- lence, Dis- perse, dis- perse, ye gal- lant men! Dis-
-teilt euch hier im Stil- len, ver- teilt euch, wack- re Män- ner, hier durch
-perse, dis- perse, in si- lence, Dis- perse, dis- perse, ye gal- lant men! Dis-
wack- re Män- ner, hier im Stil- len, ver- teilt euch, wack- re Män- ner, hier durch
-perse, ye gal- lant men! In si- lence dis- perse, dis- perse, ye gal- lant men! Dis-
Ver- teilt euch hier im Stil- len, ver- teilt euch, wack- re Män- ner, hier durch
Dis- perse, dis- perse, in si- lence dis- perse, dis- perse, ye gal- lant men! Dis-

790
*
Fl. 1, 2
pp
Ob. 1, 2
Cl. 1, 2 in A
pp
Bn. 1, 2
Hn. 1, 2 in E
Tpt. 1, 2 in E
[CHOR DER WÄCHTER DES HEIDENVOLKS]
T1
dieses Waldrevier, durch dieses ganze Waldrevier, verteilt, ver-
-perse, ye gallant men! Secure the passes round the glen: disperse, dis-
T2
dieses Waldrevier, durch dieses ganze Waldrevier, verteilt, ver-
-perse, ye gallant men! Secure the passes round the glen: disperse, dis-
B1
dieses Waldrevier, durch dieses ganze Waldrevier, verteilt, ver-
-perse, ye gallant men! Secure the passes round the glen: disperse, dis-
B2
dieses Waldrevier, durch dieses ganze Waldrevier, verteilt, ver-
-perse, ye gallant men! Secure the passes round the glen: disperse, dis-
Vn. 1
Vn. 2
Va.
Vc.
Cb.

*See Text-Genetic Remarks (I: mm. 794–97).

800
Fl. 1, 2
Ob. 1, 2
Cl. 1, 2 in A
Bn. 1, 2
Hn. 1, 2 in E
Tpt. 1, 2 in E
[CHOR DER WÄCHTER DES HEIDENVOLKS]
T1
wa- chet hier im Stil- len, im Stil- - -
si- lence there pro- tect them, in si- - -
T2
wa- chet hier im Stil- len, im Stil- -
si- lence there pro- tect them, in si- -
B1
wa- chet hier im Stil- len, im Stil- -
si- lence there pro- tect them, in si- -
B2
wa- chet hier im Stil- len, im Stil-
si- lence there pro- tect them, in si-
Vn. 1
Vn. 2
Va.
Vc.
Cb.

806
p
p
p
dim.
dim.
dim.
1
pp
a 2
pp
-len, im Stil- - len!
-lence . . . in si- - lence . . .
-len, im Stil- - len!
-lence . . . in si- - lence . . .
-len, im Stil- - len!
-lence . . . in si- - lence . . .
pp
-len, im Stil-
-lence . . . in si-
arco
pp
arco
pp
arco
pp
arco
pp
arco
pp

812
Fl. 1, 2
Ob. 1, 2
Cl. 1, 2 in A
Bn. 1, 2
Hn. 1, 2 in E
Tpt. 1, 2 in E
[CHOR DER WÄCHTER DES HEIDENVOLKS]
T1
T2
B1
B2
- len!
- lence . . .
Vn. 1
Vn. 2
Va.
Vc.
Cb.
pizz.

No. 2

*See Text-Genetic Remarks and Appendix II.1.

[in D]
[Strophe 7]
Recitativo
Hn. 1, 2 in E
Druide [1]
Vn. 1
Vn. 2
Va.
Vc.
Cb.
Die- se dump-fen Pfaf-fen-chris- ten,
Should our Chris-tian foes as- sail us,
lasst uns keck sie ü- ber-lis- ten!
aid a scheme that may a- vail us!
Mit dem Teu- fel, den sie fa- beln, wol-len wir sie selbst er- schre-cken.
Feign-ing De- mons whom they fa- ble, We will scare the big- ot rab- ble.
Tempo. Con moto
Mit dem Teu- fel, den sie fa- beln,
Feign-ing De- mons whom they fa- ble,
ad lib.
wol- len wir sie selbst er-schre-cken.
We will scare the big- ot rab- ble.

[Allegro moderato]
21
tr
p
[Allegro moderato]
Kommt! Kommt! Kommt! Mit Za- cken und mit
Come! Come! Come with flap- pers, Fire and
[Allegro moderato]
stacc.
pp
27
Ga- beln und mit Glut und Klap- per- stö- cken lär- men wir bei nächt'-ger Wei- le durch die
clap- pers, Hop, with hop- sticks, Brooms and mop- sticks; Thro' the night-gloom lead and fol- low In and
32
in D
2
mf
en- gen Fel- sen- stre- cken. Kommt! Kommt! Kommt mit Za- cken und mit
out each rock- y hol- low. Come! Come! Come with flap- pers, Fire and
Kommt! Kommt mit Za- cken und mit
Come! Come! with flap- pers, Fire and
Kommt! Kommt mit Za- cken und mit
Come! Come! with flap- pers, Fire and

38
Hn. 1, 2 in D
Timp.
Druide [1]
[CHOR DER WÄCHTER DES HEIDENVOLKS]
T
B
Va.
Vc.
Cb.
p
stacc.
Ga- beln und mit Glut und Klap- per- stö- cken lär- men wir bei nächt'-ger Wei- le durch die
clap- pers, Hop, with hop- sticks, Brooms and mop- sticks; Thro' the night-gloom lead and fol- low In and
J
43
Fl. 1, 2
Cl. 1, 2 in B♭
Hn. 1, 2 in D
Timp.
Druide [1]
T
B
Va.
Vc.
Cb.
leggiero
[leggiero]
tr
p
cresc.
en- gen Fel- sen- stre- cken. Kommt! Kommt! Kommt mit
out each rock- y hol- low. Come! Come! Come with
en- gen Fel- sen- stre- cken. Kommt! Kommt mit
out each rock- y hol- low. Come! Come with

48
leggiero
leggiero
p
p
cresc.
cresc.
Za- cken und mit Ga- beln und mit Glut und Klap- per- stö- cken lär- men
flap- pers, Fire and clap- pers, Hop, with hop- sticks, Brooms and mop- sticks; Thro' the
cresc.
Za- cken und mit Ga- beln und mit Glut und Klap- per- stö- cken lär- men
flap- pers, Fire and clap- pers, Hop, with hop- sticks, Brooms and mop- sticks; Thro' the
cresc.
Za- cken und mit Ga- beln und mit Glut und Klap- per- stö- cken lär- men
flap pers, Fire and clap- pers, Hop, with hop- sticks, Brooms and mop- sticks; Thro' the
cresc.
cresc.
cresc.

*See Text-Genetic Remarks (II: mm. 54–55) and Appendix II.2.

K
56
tr
p
più f
-cken. Kommt! Kommt!
-low. Come! Come!
più f
-cken. Kommt! Kommt!
-low. Come! Come!
più f
cken. Kommt! Kommt! Kommt mit
-low. Come! Come! Come with
stacc.
pp
stacc.
pp
pp

59
Fl. 1, 2
Ob. 1, 2
Cl. 1, 2 in B♭
Bn. 1, 2
Hn. 1, 2 in D
Timp.
Druide [1]
Kommt mit Za- cken und mit Ga- beln und mit
Come with flap- pers, Fire and clap- pers, Hop, with
[CHOR DER WÄCHTER DES HEIDENVOLKS]
T
Kommt mit Za- cken und mit Ga- beln und mit
Come with flap- pers, Fire and clap- pers, Hop, with
B
Za- cken und mit Ga- beln und mit Glut und Klap- per-
flap- pers, Fire and clap- pers, Hop, with hop- sticks, Brooms and
Vn. 1
sempre pp
Vn. 2
sempre pp
Va.
Vc.
Cb.

62
Glut und Klap- per- stö- cken, kommt mit Za- cken und mit
hop- sticks, Brooms and mop- sticks; Come with flap- pers, Fire and
Glut und Klap- per- stö- cken, kommt mit Za- cken und mit
hop- sticks, Brooms and mop- sticks; Come with flap- pers, Fire and
-stö- cken, lär- men wir bei nächt'- ger Wei- le durch die
mop- sticks; Thro' the night- gloom lead and fol- low In and

65
Fl. 1, 2
Ob. 1, 2
Cl. 1, 2 in B♭
Bn. 1, 2
Hn. 1, 2 in D
Tpt. 1, 2 in D
soli
Timp.
Druide [1]
Ga- beln durch die en- gen Fel- sen-
clap- pers, In and out each rock- y
[CHOR DER WÄCHTER DES HEIDENVOLKS]
T
Ga- beln durch die en- gen Fel- sen-
clap- pers, In and out each rock- y
B
en- gen Fel- sen- stre- -
out each rock- y hol- -
Vn. 1
Vn. 2
Va.
Vc.
Cb.

68
in C
tr
-stre- cken, durch die en-
hol- low, In and out
-stre- cken, durch die en-
hol- low, In and out
-cken, durch die en-
-low, In and out

71
Fl. 1, 2
Ob. 1, 2
Cl. 1, 2 in B♭
Bn. 1, 2
Timp.
Druide [1]
- gen Fel- sen- stre- cken. Kommt mit
each rock- y hol- low. Come with
[CHOR DER WÄCHTER DES HEIDENVOLKS]
T
- gen Fel- sen- stre- cken. Kommt mit
each rock- y hol- low. Come with
B
- gen Fel- sen- stre- cken. Kommt mit Za- cken und mit
each rock- y hol- low. Come with flap- pers, Fire and
Vn. 1
Vn. 2
Va.
Vc.
Cb.

74
Za- cken durch die Fel- sen-
flap- pers, Thro' each rock- y
Za- cken durch die Fel- sen-
flap- pers, Thro' each rock- y
Ga- beln, kommt mit Za- cken durch die Fel- sen-
clap- pers, Come with flap- pers, Thro' each rock- y

77
Fl. 1, 2
Ob. 1, 2
Cl. 1, 2 in B♭
fp
Bn. 1, 2
fp
Timp.
sfz
Druide [1]
f
-stre- cken. Kauz und Eu- le, heul' in
hol- low. Owls and ra- vens, Howl with
[CHOR DER WÄCHTER DES HEIDENVOLKS]
T
f
-stre- cken. Kauz und Eu- le, heul' in
hol- low. Owls and ra- vens, Howl with
B
f
-stre- cken. Kauz und Eu- le, heul' in
hol- low. Owls and ra- vens, Howl with
Vn. 1
Vn. 2
Va.
sf
Vc.
sf pp
Cb.
sf pp

80
p
sf
un- ser Rund- - ge- heu- le, un- ser
us and scare the Cra- vens, scare the
sf
un- ser Rund- - ge- heu- le, un- ser
us and scare the Cra- vens, scare the
sf
un- ser Rund- - ge- heu- le, un- ser
us and scare the Cra- vens, scare the
pp

83
Fl. 1, 2
Ob. 1, 2
Cl. 1, 2 in B♭
Bn. 1, 2
Timp.
Druide [1]
Rund- ge- heu- -
Cra- vens! Come!
[CHOR DER WÄCHTER DES HEIDENVOLKS]
T
Rund- ge- heu- -
Cra- vens! Come!
B
Rund- ge- heu- -
Cra- vens! Come!
Vn. 1
Vn. 2
Va.
Vc.
Cb.

86
pp
in C
tr
pp
sempre pp
f
-le!
Come!
Kommt! Kommt! Kommt!
Come! Come! Come!
ff
-le!
Come!
Kommt! Kommt!
Come! Come!
ff
-le!
Come!
Kommt! Kommt!
Come! Come!
pp
pp

90
[Strophe 8]
Allegro di molto
Fl. 1, 2
Ob. 1, 2
Cl. 1, 2 in C
in C
Bn. 1, 2
a 2
Hn. 1, 2 in D
a 2
Tpt. 1, 2 in C
in C
Timp.
in E-A
Druide [1]
Allegro di molto
Kommt!
Come!
[CHOR DER WÄCHTER DES HEIDENVOLKS]
T
Kommt!
Come!
B
Kommt!
Come!
Allegro di molto
Vn. 1
Vn. 2
Va.
Vc.
Cb.
ff

96
p
a 2
mf
stacc.
a 2
mf
stacc.
p
pizz.
p
pizz.
p

102
[simile]
Fl. 1, 2
mf
Ob. 1, 2
a 2
mf
Cl. 1, 2
in C
mf
[simile]
Bn. 1, 2
a 2
mf [stacc.]
Hn. 1, 2
in D
a 2
f
Tpt. 1, 2
in C
f
Timp.
Vn. 1
f
sf
Vn. 2
f
sf
Va.
f
sf
Vc.
arco
f
Cb.
arco
f

108
stacc.
cresc.
f
p
a 2
cresc. [al]
divisi
[unisono]
pizz.

113
a 2
Fl. 1, 2
cresc. al
ff
Ob. 1, 2
cresc. al
ff
Cl. 1, 2
in C
cresc. al
ff
Bn. 1, 2
cresc. al
ff
Hn. 1, 2
in D
a 2
cresc. al
ff
Tpt. 1, 2
in C
stacc.
ff
Timp.
[CHOR DES HEIDENVOLKS]
S
A
T
B
Vn. 1
ff
Vn. 2
ff
Va.
ff
Vc.
Cb.

118
mf
f
Kommt mit Za- cken und mit
Come with flap- pers, Fire and
f
Kommt mit Za- cken und mit
Come with flap- pers, Fire and
con fuoco
f
con fuoco
f
con fuoco
f
mf
[con fuoco]
cresc. f
mf
[con fuoco]
cresc. f

124
Fl. 1, 2
Ob. 1, 2
Cl. 1, 2 in C
p solo
Bn. 1, 2
p
Hn. 1, 2 in D
Tpt. 1, 2 in C
Timp.
[CHOR DES HEIDENVOLKS]
T
Ga- beln, wie der Teu- fel, den sie fa- beln, und mit wil- den Klap- per- stö- cken durch die
clap- pers, Feign-ing De- mons whom they fa- ble, Come with hop- sticks, Brooms and mop- sticks, In and
B
Ga- beln, wie der Teu- fel, den sie fa- beln, und mit wil- den Klap- per- stö- cken durch die
clap- pers, Feign-ing De- mons whom they fa- ble, Come with hop- sticks, Brooms and mop- sticks, In and
Vn. 1
cresc. sempre
Vn. 2
cresc. sempre
Va.
cresc. sempre
Vc.
cresc. sempre
Cb.
cresc. sempre

L
130
ff
ff
ff
ff
ff
ff
tr
ff
f
lee- ren Fel- - sen- stre- cken!
out each rock- - y hol- low!
f
lee- ren Fel- - sen- stre- cken!
out each rock- - y hol low!

136
Fl. 1, 2
Ob. 1, 2
Cl. 1, 2
in C
Bn. 1, 2
Hn. 1, 2
in D
Tpt. 1, 2
in C
tr
Timp.
[CHOR DES HEIDENVOLKS]
T
ff
Kauz und Kauz
Owls and Owls
Kauz und Eu- le, Kauz
Owls and ra- vens, Owls
B
ff
Kauz und Eu- le, Kauz
Owls and ra- vens, Owls
Vn. 1
ff
Vn. 2
ff
Va.
ff
Vc.
ff
Cb.
ff

*See Critical Notes (II: mm. 142–50).

*See Text-Genetic Remarks (II: mm. 149–50) and Appendix II.3.

152
M
a 2
Kommt mit Za- cken und mit Ga- beln,
Come with flap- pers, Fire and clap- pers,
Kommt mit Za- cken und mit Ga- beln,
Come with flap- pers, Fire and clap- pers,
Rund- ge- heu- le! Kommt!
scare the Cra- vens! Come!
Rund- ge- heu- le! Kommt!
scare the Cra- vens! Come!

158
Fl. 1, 2
Ob. 1, 2
Cl. 1, 2 in C
Bn. 1, 2
Hn. 1, 2 in D
Tpt. 1, 2 in C
[CHOR DES HEIDENVOLKS]
S
wie der Teu- fel, den sie fa- beln, kommt, kommt, Kommt! und mit wil- den
Feign-ing De- mons whom they fa- ble, Come! Come! Come! Come with hop- sticks,
A
wie der Teu- fel, den sie fa- beln, kommt, kommt, Kommt! und mit wil- den
Feign-ing De- mons whom they fa- ble, Come! Come! Come! Come with hop- sticks,
Vn. 1
Vn. 2
Va.
Vc.
Cb.

164
sfp
sf
Klap- per- stö- cken durch die lee- ren Fel- sen- stre- cken! Kommt, kommt,
Brooms and mop- sticks, In and out each rock- y hol- low! Come! Come!
Klap- per- stö- cken durch die lee- ren Fel- sen- stre- cken! Kommt, kommt,
Brooms and mop- sticks, In and out each rock- y hol- low! Come! Come!

169
Fl. 1, 2
Ob. 1, 2
Cl. 1, 2 in C
Bn. 1, 2
Hn. 1, 2 in D
Tpt. 1, 2 in C
a 2
stacc.
[CHOR DES HEIDENVOLKS]
S
kommt! Kauz und Eu- le, heul' in un- ser Rund- ge-
Come! Owls and ra- vens, Howl with us and scare the
A
kommt! Kauz und Eu- le, heul' in un- ser Rund- ge-
Come! Owls and ra- vens, Howl with us and scare the
Vn. 1
Vn. 2
Va.
Vc.
Cb.

175
p
p
2
p
-heu- le! Kommt, kommt, kommt! Kauz und Eu- le, heul' in
Cra- vens! Come! Come! Come! Owls and ra- vens, Howl with
-heu- le! Kommt, kommt, kommt! Kauz und Eu- le, heul' in
Cra- vens! Come! Come! Come! Owls and ra- vens, Howl with
stacc. sempre
stacc. sempre
stacc. [sempre]

181
Fl. 1, 2
Ob. 1, 2
Cl. 1, 2 in C
Bn. 1, 2
Hn. 1, 2 in D
Tpt. 1, 2 in C
Timp.
[CHOR DES HEIDENVOLKS]
S
un- ser Rund- ge- heu- le! Kommt, kommt, kommt! Kommt mit
us and scare the Cra- vens! Come! Come! Come! Come with
A
un- ser Rund- ge- heu- le! Kommt, kommt, kommt! Kommt mit
us and scare the Cra- vens! Come! Come! Come! Come with
T
Kauz
Owls
B
Kauz
Owls
Vn. 1
Vn. 2
Va.
Vc.
Cb.

187
Za- cken und mit Ga- beln wie der Teu- fel, den sie fa- beln, kommt, kommt,
flap- pers, Fire and clap- pers, Feign- ing De- mons whom they fa- ble, Come! Come!
Za- cken und mit Ga- beln wie der Teu- fel, den sie fa- beln, kommt, kommt,
flap- pers, Fire and clap- pers, Feign- ing De- mons whom they fa- ble, Come! Come!
und Eu- le, heul'
and ra vens, Howl
und Eu- le, heul'
and ra- vens, Howl

193
Fl. 1, 2
Ob. 1, 2
Cl. 1, 2 in C
Bn. 1, 2
Hn. 1, 2 in D
Tpt. 1, 2 in C
Timp.
S
A
T
B
[CHOR DES HEIDENVOLKS]
Vn. 1
Vn. 2
Va.
Vc.
Cb.
più f
[più] f
fp
più f
pp
pizz.
kommt! und mit wilden Klap- per- stö- cken durch die lee- ren
Come! Come with hop- sticks, Brooms and mop- sticks, In and out each
in unser Rund- ge- heu- le,
with us and scare the Cra- vens!

199
p
stacc.
1
p
stacc.
p
tr
p
Fel- sen-stre- cken! Kommt! Kommt! Kommt! Kommt mit Za- cken und mit Ga- beln.
rock- y hol- low! Come! Come! Come! Come with flap- pers, Fire and clap- pers,
Fel- sen-stre- cken! Kommt! Kommt! Kommt! Kommt mit Za- cken und mit Ga- beln.
rock- y hol- low! Come! Come! Come! Come with flap- pers, Fire and clap- pers,
p
heul' in un- ser Rund- ge- heu-
Howl with us and scare the Cra-
p
heul' in un- ser Rund- ge- heu-
Howl with us and scare the Cra-
sf
sf
sf
sf
p
sf
sf
arco
p
sf
sf
arco
p
sf
sf

*See Text-Genetic Remarks (II: mm. 212–19).

213
Eu- le, Kauz und Eu- le
ra- vens, Owls and ra- vens,
Kommt mit Za- cken, kommt mit Ga- beln,
Come with flap- pers, Come with clap- pers,
mit Za- - cken und mit Ga- -
with flap- - pers, and with clap- -
kommt mit Za- - cken
Come with flap- - pers,
cresc.

220
Fl. 1, 2
Ob. 1, 2
Cl. 1, 2 in C
a 2
Bn. 1, 2
Hn. 1, 2 in D
Tpt. 1, 2 in C
Timp.
[CHOR DES HEIDENVOLKS]
S
wie der Teu- fel,
Feign- ing De- mons
A
[Kommt!]
Come!
wie der
Feign- - ing
T
-beln,
-pers,
wie der Teu- fel, den sie
Feign- ing De- mons whom they
B
wie der Teu- fel, den sie fa- -
Feign- ing De- mons whom they fa- -
Vn. 1
Vn. 2
cresc.
Va.
cresc.
Vc.
cresc.
Cb.
cresc.

226
a 2
f
cresc.
tr
p
sf
den sie fa- beln, den sie
whom they fa- ble, whom they
Teu- fel, den sie fa-
De- mons whom they fa-
fa- beln, den sie fa-
fa- ble, whom they fa-
beln!
ble!
cresc. al

232
N
Fl. 1, 2
Ob. 1, 2
Cl. 1, 2 in C
Bn. 1, 2
Hn. 1, 2 in D
Tpt. 1, 2 in C
Timp.
[CHOR DES HEIDENVOLKS]
S
fa- - beln!
fa- - ble!
A
- - beln!
- - ble!
T
-beln! Kommt mit Za- cken und mit Ga- beln, kommt, kommt,
-ble! Come with flap- pers, Fire and clap- pers, Come, Come,
B
Kommt! Kommt mit Za- cken und mit Ga- beln, kommt, kommt,
Come! Come with flap- pers, Fire and clap- pers, Come, Come,
Vn. 1
Vn. 2
Va.
Vc.
Cb.

238
a 2
Kauz und Eu- le, heul' in un- ser Rund- ge- heu- le! Kommt!
Owls and ra- vens, Howl with us __ and scare ______ the Cra- vens! Come!
Kauz und Eu- le, heul' in un- ser Rund- ge- heu- le! Kommt!
Owls and ra- vens, Howl with us __ and scare ______ the Cra- vens! Come!
kommt! Kommt ____ mit Za- cken und mit
Come! Come ______ with flap- pers, Fire and
kommt! Kommt ____ mit Za- cken und mit
Come! Come ______ with flap- pers, Fire and

244
Fl. 1, 2
Ob. 1, 2
Cl. 1, 2 in C
Bn. 1, 2
Hn. 1, 2 in D
Tpt. 1, 2 in C
Timp.
[CHOR DES HEIDENVOLKS]
S
A
T
B
Vn. 1
Vn. 2
Va.
Vc.
Cb.
a 2
Kauz und Eu- le heul' in un- ser Rund- ge- heu- le!
Owls and ra- vens, Howl with us and scare the Cra- vens!
Ga- beln Kommt! Kommt! Kommt!
clap- pers, Come! Come! Come!

250
a 2
Heul'
Howl
Kommt!
Come!
Heul'
Howl
Kauz
Owls
Heul'
Howl
Kauz
Owls
Heul'
Howl
Kauz
Owls
Heul'
Howl
Kauz
Owls

257
Fl. 1, 2
Ob. 1, 2
Cl. 1, 2 in C
Bn. 1, 2
Hn. 1, 2 in D
Tpt. 1, 2 in C
Timp.
tr
[CHOR DES HEIDENVOLKS]
S
A
T
B
und Eu- - le heul' in un- ser Rund- ge-
and ra- - vens, Howl with us and scare the
Vn. 1
Vn. 2
Va.
Vc.
Cb.

264
-heu- le! Heul'
Cra- vens! Howl
sf
-heu- le! Kauz und Eu- le, heul' in
Cra- vens! Owls and ra- vens, Howl with
-heu- le! Heul'
Cra- vens! Howl
sf
-heu- le! Kauz und Eu- le, heul' in
Cra- vens! Owls and ra- vens, Howl with

272
O
Fl. 1, 2
Ob. 1, 2
Cl. 1, 2 in C
Bn. 1, 2
mf
Hn. 1, 2 in D
ff
Tpt. 1, 2 in C
a 2
ff
Timp.
tr
ff
[CHOR DES HEIDENVOLKS]
S
A
un- ser Rund- ge- heu- - le!
us and scare the Cra- - vens!
T
B
un- ser Rund- ge- heu- - le!
us and scare the Cra- - vens!
Vn. 1
ff
Vn. 2
ff
Va.
ff
Vc.
ff
Cb.
ff

*See Text-Genetic Remarks (II: mm. 283–84) and Appendix II.4.

287
Fl. 1, 2
1
[CHOR DES HEIDENVOLKS]
S
A
Ga- beln und mit Glut und Klap- per- stö- cken, durch die lee- ren Fel- sen-
clap- pers, Come with hop- sticks, Brooms and mop- sticks, In and out each rock- y
Vn. 1
Vn. 2
Va.
Vc.
Cb.
295
Ob. 1, 2
1 solo
Hn. 1, 2 in D
[CHOR DES HEIDENVOLKS]
S
A
-stre- cken lär- men wir bei nächt- ger Wei- le.
hol- low! Thro' the night- gloom lead and fol- low.
T
B
Kauz und Eu- le,
Owls and ra- vens,
Vn. 1
Vn. 2
Va.
Vc.
Cb.

302
p
[cresc.]
1
p
cresc.
p [cresc.]
cresc.
cresc.
Kauz und Eu- le, heul' in
Owls and ra- vens, Howl with
p
cresc.
Kauz und Eu- le, Kauz und Eu- le, heul' in
Owls and ra- vens, owls and ra- vens, Howl with
p
cresc.
Kauz und Eu- le, heul' in un- ser Rund- ge- heu- le!
Owls and ra- vens, Howl with us and scare the Cra- vens!
cresc.
Kauz und Eu- le, heul' in un- ser Rund- ge- heu- le!
owls and ra- vens, Howl with us and scare the Cra vens!
cresc. sempre al
cresc. sempre al
cresc. sempre al
cresc. sempre al
cresc. sempre al

309
Fl. 1
Fl. 2
Ob. 1
Ob. 2
Cl. 1 in C
Cl. 2 in C
Bn. 1, 2
Hn. 1, 2 in D
Tpt. 1, 2 in C
Timp.
S
A
T
B
Vn. 1
Vn. 2
Va.
Vc.
Cb.
[CHOR DES HEIDENVOLKS]
cresc.
mf [cresc.]
f [cresc.]
mf cresc.
ff
a 2
ff possibile
in B♭-E
tr
un- ser Rund- ge- heu- le! Kauz und Eu-
us and scare the Cra- vens! Owls and ra-
un- ser Rund- ge- heu- le! und Eu-
us and scare the Cra- vens! and ra-
heul' in un- ser Rund- ge- heu- le! Heul'!
Howl with us and scare the cra- vens! Howl!

*See Text-Genetic Remarks (II: mm. 317–23) and Appendix II.5.

323
Fl. 1, 2
Ob. 1, 2
Cl. 1, 2 in C
Bn. 1, 2
Hn. 1, 2 in D
Tpt. 1, 2 in C
[CHOR DES HEIDENVOLKS]
S
Za- cken, kommt mit Ga- beln,
flap- pers, Fire and clap- pers,
A
Za- cken, kommt mit Ga- beln,
flap- pers, Fire and clap- pers,
T
kommt mit wil- den Klap- per-
Come, with hop- sticks, Brooms and
B
kommt mit wil- den Klap- per-
Come with hop- sticks, Brooms and
Vn. 1
Vn. 2
Va.
Vc.
Cb.

329
a 2
durch die lee- ren Fel- sen- stre- cken!
In and out each rock- y hol- low.
durch die lee- ren Fel- sen- stre- cken!
In and out each rock- y hol- low.
-stö- cken
mop- sticks;
-stö- cken
mop- sticks;
Kauz
Owls

335
Fl. 1, 2
Ob. 1, 2
Cl. 1, 2 in C
Bn. 1, 2
Hn. 1, 2 in D
Tpt. 1, 2 in C
[CHOR DES HEIDENVOLKS]
S
Kauz und
Owls and
A
Kauz und Eu- -
Owls and ra- -
T
Kauz und Eu- le, heul',
Owls and ra- vens, Howl,
B
und Eu- le, Kauz und Eu- - le,
and ra- vens, owls and ra- - vens,
Vn. 1
Vn. 2
Va.
Vc.
Cb.

342
a 2
tr
[a 2]
Eu- le, heul' in un- ser Rund- - ge- heu-
ra- vens, Howl with us and scare the Cra-
- - le, heul'!
- - vens, Howl
heul' in un- ser Rund- ge- heu- le! Kauz
Howl with us and scare the Cra- vens! Owls
heul'! Kauz und Eu- le heul',
Howl! Owls and ra- vens, Howl,

*See Text-Genetic Remarks (II: mm. 352–75).

356
a 2
a 2
le, Kauz
vens, owls
le
vens,
heul' in un- ser
Howl with us and
Eu- le, Kauz und Eu- le, heul'
ra- vens, owls and ra- vens, Howl

*See Text-Genetic Remarks (II: mm. 364–65) and Appendix II.6.

366
sf
a 2
tr
- - - le, Kommt!
- - - vens, Come!
- - - le! Kommt! Kommt!
- - - vens! Come! Come!
- - ser Rund- ge-
and scare the

Q
371
Fl. 1, 2
Ob. 1, 2
Cl. 1, 2 in C
Bn. 1, 2
Hn. 1, 2 in D
a 2
Tpt. 1, 2 in C
Timp.
[CHOR DES HEIDENVOLKS]
S
Kommt! Kommt! Kommt! Kauz und Eu- le, Kauz und
Come! Come! Come! Owls and ra- vens, owls and
A
Kommt! Kommt! Kommt! Kauz und Eu- le, Kauz und
Come! Come! Come! Owls and ra- vens, owls and
T
Kommt! Kommt! Kommt! Kauz und Eu- le, Kauz und
Come! Come! Come! Owls and ra- vens, owls and
B
-heu- - le! Kauz und Eu- le, Kauz und
Cra- - vens! Owls and ra- vens, owls and
Vn. 1
Vn. 2
Va.
Vc.
Cb.

377
sf
a 2
ffsf
ff
Eu- le, heul' in un- ser Rund- ge- heul'!
ra- vens, Howl with us and scare the Cra- vens!
Eu- le, heul' in un- ser Rund- ge- heul'!
ra- vens, Howl with us and scare the Cra- vens!
Eu- le, heul' in un- ser Rund- ge- heul'!
ra- vens, Howl with us and scare the Cra- vens!
Eu- le, heul' in un- ser Rund- ge- heul'!
ra- vens, Howl with us and scare the Cra- vens!

383
Fl. 1, 2
Ob. 1, 2
Cl. 1, 2 in C
Bn. 1, 2
Hn. 1, 2 in D
Tpt. 1, 2 in C
Timp.
[CHOR DES HEIDENVOLKS]
S
A
T
B
Kommt! Come!
Vn. 1
Vn. 2
Va.
Vc.
Cb.

*These measures half as fast as the preceding ones.

*See Text-Genetic Remarks (II: mm. 394–95) and Appendix II.7.

*See Text-Genetic Remarks (II: mm. 397–98) and Appendix II.7.

[Strophe 9]

Più Lento

403
p
sfz
sf
p
sf
sf
f
sf
sf
f
sf
sf
f
(tr)
tr
sempre dim.
f
f
p
f
f
p
f
f
p
f

407
Fl. 1, 2
Ob. 1, 2
Cl. 1, 2 in C
Bn. 1, 2
Hn. 1, 2 in C
in C
Tpt. 1, 2 in C
Trb. 1, 2
Trb. 3
Druide [2]
So weit ge- bracht,
Re- strain'd by might,
Vn. 1
Vn. 2
Va.
Vc.
Cb.

411
pp
p
p
p
dass wir bei Nacht All-
We now by night, In
p
p
p
p
sempre p
sf sf
p
sempre p

416
Trb. 1, 2
dim.
Trb. 3
[dim.]
Druide [2]
-va- ter heim- lich ___ sin- - gen!
se- cret here a- dore ___ Thee!
Vn. 1
dim.
Vn. 2
dim.
Va.
dim.
Vc.
p
Cb.
p
421
Cl. 1, 2 in C
p e dolce
dolce
Bn. 1, 2
p e dolce
Druide [2]
dolce
Doch ist es Tag, so- bald man mag ein rei- nes ___ Herz dir
Still it is day When e'er we pray And hum- bly ___ bow be-
Vn. 1
p dolce
Vn. 2
p
Va.
p
Vc.
p
Cb.
p

424
S
brin- gen.
-fore Thee!
Doch ist es Tag, so- bald man mag ein
Still it is day When e'er we pray And
Doch ist es Tag, so- bald man mag ein
Still it is day When e'er we pray And

427
Fl. 1, 2
Ob. 1, 2
Cl. 1, 2 in C
Bn. 1, 2
Hn. 1, 2 in C
Tpt. 1, 2 in C
Trb. 1, 2
Trb. 3
Druide [2]
CHOR DER DRUIDEN
T
B
Vn. 1
Vn. 2
Va.
Vc.
Cb.
dim.
p
so- bald man mag ein
When e'er we pray And
rei- nes Herz dir brin- gen.
hum- bly bow be- fore Thee!

430
p dolce
p
rei- nes Herz dir brin- gen.
hum- bly bow be- fore Thee!

434
Fl. 1, 2
Ob. 1, 2
Cl. 1, 2
in C
Bn. 1, 2
Hn. 1, 2
in C
Tpt. 1, 2
in C
Trb. 1, 2
Trb. 3
Timp.
Druide [2]
Du kannst zwar heut, und man- che
Thou canst as- suage Our Foe- men's
Vn. 1
Vn. 2
Va.
Vc.
Cb.

438
p
p
p
p poco cresc.
tr
pp
cresc.
Zeit, dem Fein- de viel er- lau- ben. Die Flam- me
rage, And shield us from their ter- rors, The flame as-
p
divisi
cresc.

441
Fl. 1, 2
Ob. 1, 2
cresc.
Cl. 1, 2 in C
Bn. 1, 2
mf
cresc. sempre sino al
Hn. 1, 2 in C
Tpt. 1, 2 in C
cresc.
Trb. 1, 2
Trb. 3
poco cresc.
Timp.
tr
p
Druide [2]
cresc.
rei- nigt sich vom Rauch: So rei- nig' un- sern
-pires! The smoke re- tires! Thus clear our Faith from
Vn. 1
p
cresc.
Vn. 2
p
cresc.
[unisono]
Va.
p
cresc.
Vc.
p
sf
cresc. sempre al
Cb.
p
sf
cresc. sempre al

444
cresc. sino al
Glau- ben! Und raubt man uns den al- ten Brauch:
er- rors: Our cus- toms quell'd, Our rights with- held,
sino
sino

447
Fl. 1, 2
Ob. 1, 2
Cl. 1, 2 in C
soli
dolce
Bn. 1, 2
Hn. 1, 2 in C
dim.
Tpt. 1, 2 in C
Trb. 1, 2
Trb. 3
Timp.
Druide [2]
cresc.
Dein Licht, wer will es rau-
Thy light shall shine for ev-
[CHOR DER DRUIDEN]
S
A
T
B
Vn. 1
molto cresc.
cresc.
Vn. 2
Va.
Vc.
Cb.

*See Text-Genetic Remarks (II: mm. 451–68) and Appendix II.8.

456
[Strophe 10]
Vivace
Fl. 1, 2
Ob. 1, 2
Cl. 1, 2 in C
Bn. 1, 2
Hn. 1, 2 in C
Tpt. 1, 2 in C
Trb. 1, 2
Trb. 3
Timp.
Druide [2]
[CHOR DER DRUIDEN]
S
A
T
B
Licht! Dein Licht, wer will es rau- ben?
light, Thy light shall shine for ev- er!
Vn. 1
Vn. 2
Va.
Vc.
Cb.
[divisi]
[unisono]
stacc.

461
pp
464
p
Hilf, ach hilf mir, Kriegs- ge-sel- le! Ach, es kommt die gan- ze Höl- le!
Help, my Com- rades, see a Le- gion, Yon- der comes from Sa- tan's re- gion!
pizz.
pp
467
Sieh, wie die ver- hex- ten Lei- ber durch und durch von Flam- me glüh'n!
See, yon group of Witch- es glid- ing to and fro' in flames ad- vanc- ing!
arco
stacc.
pp

469
Hn. 1, 2 in C
Tpt. 1, 2 in C
a 2
Trb. 1, 2
Trb. 3
[Christl.] Wächter
p
cresc.
Sieh, wie die ver- hex- ten Lei- ber durch und durch von Flam- me glüh'n! Hilf mir, ach hilf mir,
See, yon group of Witch-es glid-ing to and fro' in flames ad-vanc- ing! Help me, O help me,
Vn. 1
Vn. 2
Va.
Vc.
pp e stacc.
Cb.
pp e stacc.
471
Hn. 1, 2 in C
sf
Tpt. 1, 2 in C
sf
Trb. 1, 2
sf
Trb. 3
sf
[Christl.] Wächter
f
f
p
Kriegs- ge- sel- le! Men- schen-Wölf' und Dra- chen- Wei- ber,
my Com-pan- ions! Some on Wolves and Dra- gons rid- ing;
Vn. 1
f
p
stacc. sempre
Vn. 2
f
p
stacc. sempre
Va.
f
p
[stacc. sempre]
Vc.
f
p
[stacc. sempre]
Cb.

473
dim.
die im Flug vor- ü- ber- zie- hen! Welch ent- setz- li- ches Ge-
See, ah, See them hith- er pranc- ing! What a clatt'- ring troop of
475
-tö- se! Lasst uns, lasst uns al- le flie- hen! O- ben flammt und saust der
e- vil! Let us, Let us quick- ly fly them! Imp and dev- il Lead the
[stacc.]

477
Trb. 3
[Christl.] Wächter
p
Bö- se, aus dem Bo- den dam- pfet rings ein Höl- len-
rev- el, See them ca- per, Wrapt in clouds of lu- rid
stacc.
Vn. 1
stacc.
Vn. 2
stacc.
Va.
Vc.
[stacc.]
Cb.
479
Hn. 1, 2 in C
p
[Christl.] Wächter
-Bro- den, dam- pfet rings ein Höl- len- Bro- den. Lasst uns flie- hen! Aus dem
va- pour! Wrapt in clouds of lu- rid va- pour! Let us fly them! See them
Vn. 1
Vn. 2
Va.
Vc.
Cb.

481
T
[Strophe 11]
Bo- den dam- pfet rings ein Höl- len- Bro- den.
ca- per, Wrapt in clouds of lu- rid va- pour!
(KLEINERER CHOR)
pp
Schreck-li- che, ver- hex- te Lei-
See the hor- rid Hag- gards glid-
pp
Schreck-li- che, ver- hex- te Lei-
See the hor- rid Hag- gards glid-
pp
Schreck-li- che, ver- hex- te Lei-
See the hor- rid Hag- gards glid-
pp
Schreck-li- che, ver- hex- te Lei-
See the hor- rid Hag- gards glid-

483
Hn. 1, 2 in C
Tpt. 1, 2 in C
Trb. 1, 2
Trb. 3
Timp.
CHOR DER [CHRISTLICHEN] WÄCHTER
T1
T2
B1
B2
Vn. 1
Vn. 2
Va.
Vc.
Cb.
f
sf
tr
p
pp
-ber,
-ing,
Men-schen-Wölf' und Dra- chen- Wei-
Some on Wolves and Dra- gons rid-

485
tr
-ber! Welch ent- setz- li- ches Ge-
-ing; What a clatt'- ring troop of
-ber! Welch ent- setz- li- ches Ge-
-ing; What a clatt'- ring troop of
-ber! Welch ent- setz- li- ches Ge-
-ing; What a clatt'- ring troop of
-ber! Welch ent- setz- li- ches Ge-
-ing; What a clatt'- ring troop of
stacc.
stacc.

487
Hn. 1, 2 in C
Tpt. 1, 2 in C
Trb. 1, 2
Trb. 3
Timp.
CHOR DER [CHRISTLICHEN] WÄCHTER
T1
T2
B1
B2
cresc.
-tö- se! Sieh, da flammt, da zieht der Bö- se! Aus dem Bo- den dam- pfet
e- vil! Imp and de- vil Lead the re- vel, See them ca- per, Wrapt in
Vn. 1
Vn. 2
Va.
Vc.
Cb.

489
a 2
ff
ff
ff
tr
ff
fsf
rings ein Höl- len- Bro- den. Sieh!
clouds of lu- rid va- pour! See!
ffsf
fsf
rings ein Höl- len- Bro- den. Sieh!
clouds of lu- rid va- pour! See!
ffsf
fsf
rings ein Höl- len- Bro- den. Sieh!
clouds of lu- rid va- pour! See!
ffsf
fsf
rings cin Höl- len- Bro- den. Sieh!
clouds of lu- rid va- pour! See!
ffsf
f
pp
f
pp
divisi
f
pizz.
f
ff
pp
pizz.
ff
pp

491
Hn. 1, 2 in C
Trb. 1, 2
Trb. 3
Timp.
tr
T1
T2
B1
B2
CHOR DER [CHRISTLICHEN] WÄCHTER
Sieh! da flammt, da
See! Imp and dev- il Lead the
p
Vn. 1
Vn. 2
Va.
Vc.
Cb.
stacc.
[stacc.]
f
sempre pizz.

493
mf
mf
zieht, da flammt,
rev- el, Imp and dev- il
zieht, da flammt,
rev- el, Imp and dev- il
p
cresc.
zieht, der Bö- se! Sieh, da zieht der Bö- se! Lasst uns al- le
rev- el, Imp and dev- il See them hith- er pranc- ing! Let us quick- ly
495
p
Lasst uns flie- hen! Lasst uns flie- hen! Lasst uns al- le
Let us fly them! Let us fly them! Let us quick- ly
p
flie- hen! Lasst uns al- le flieh'n!
fly them! Let us quick- ly fly!
pp
pp
pp
pp
pp

497
Hn. 1, 2 in C
CHOR DER [CHRISTL.] WÄCHTER
T
flieh'n! Lasst uns al- le flieh'n! Lasst uns flie- hen!
fly! Let us quick- ly fly! Let us fly them!
B
Lasst uns al- le flieh'n! Lasst uns al- le, al- le flie- hen! Lasst uns
Let us quick- ly fly! Let us quick- ly, quick- ly fly them! Let us
Vn. 1
Vn. 2
Va.
Vc.
Cb.
499
Hn. 1, 2 in C
Tpt. 1, 2 in C
Trb. 1, 2
Trb. 3
Timp.
CHOR DER [CHRISTL.] WÄCHTER
T
Lasst uns flie- hen! Lasst uns flie- hen!
Let us fly them! Let us fly them!
B
al- le, al- le flie- hen! Lasst uns flie- hen!
quick- ly, quick- ly fly them! Let us fly them!
Vn. 1
Vn. 2
Va.
Vc.
Cb.

501
soli
stacc.
p
stacc.
pp
[stacc.]
p
pp
Schreck- li- che, ver- hex- te Lei-
See, yon group of Witch- es glid-
pp
Schreck- li- che, ver- hex- te Lei-
See, yon group of Witch- es glid-
pp
pp
pp

503
Fl. 1, 2
Ob. 1, 2
Cl. 1, 2 in C
CHOR DER [CHRISTL.] WÄCHTER
T
- ber! Lasst uns flie- hen!
- ing, Let us fly them!
B
- ber! Lasst uns flie- hen!
- ing, Let us fly them!
Vn. 1
sempre stacc.
Vn. 2
[sempre stacc.]
Va.
[sempre stacc.]
Vc.
arco
pp
stacc.
Cb.
505
T
Lasst uns flie- hen, al- le flie- hen!
Let us fly them, quick- ly fly them!
B
Lasst uns flie- hen, al- le flie- hen!
Let us fly them, quick- ly fly them!
Vn. 1
stacc.
pp
Vn. 2
stacc.
pp
Va.
stacc. [sempre]
pp
Vc.
stacc. sempre
pp
Cb.
arco
stacc. sempre
pp

507
Sieh, da flammt, da zieht der Bö- se! Aus dem
Imp and dev- il Lead the rev- el, See them
Sieh, da flammt, da zieht der Bö- se! Aus dem
Imp and dev- il Lead the rev- el, See them
509
Bo- den dam- pfet rings ein Höl- len- Bro-
ca- per, Wrapt in clouds of lu- rid va-
Bo- den dam- pfet rings ein Höl- len- Bro-
ca- per, Wrapt in clouds of lu- rid va-

*See Text-Genetic Remarks (II: mm. 512–15) and Appendix II.9.

513
fsf
fsf
fsf
p
fleh'n! Lasst uns flieh'n! Lasst uns, lasst uns al- le
fly! Let us fly! Let us, let us quick- ly
p
flieh'n! Lasst uns, lasst uns al- le
fly! Let us, let us quick- ly
p
flieh'n! Lasst uns flieh'n! Lasst uns, lasst uns al- le
fly! Let us fly! Let us, let us quick- ly
p
flieh'n! Lasst uns flieh'n! Lasst uns, lasst uns al- le
fly! Let us fly! Let us, let us quick- ly
dim.
515
pp
flich'n! Lasst uns flich'n!
fly! Let us fly!
pp
flieh'n! Lasst uns flieh'n!
fly! Let us fly!
pp
flieh'n! Lasst uns flieh'n!
fly! Let us fly!
pp
flieh'n! Lasst uns
fly! Let us
pp

U [Strophe 12]
517
Andante come prima
Fl. 1, 2
Ob. 1, 2
Cl. 1, 2 in C
Bn. 1, 2
Hn. 1, 2 in C
Tpt. 1, 2 in C
Trb. 1, 2
Trb. 3
Timp.
FRAUENCHOR
DER GANZE MÄNNERCHOR
CHOR DER DRUIDEN [UND DES HEIDENVOLKS]
S
A
T
B
flieh'n! Die Flam- me rei- nigt sich vom Rauch: so
fly! Un- cloud- ed now, the flame is bright! Thus
Vn. 1
Vn. 2
Va.
Vc.
Cb.

520
tenuto
tenuto
dolce
p
dolce
p
tenuto
tenuto
tr
mf
dim.
p
Die Flam- me rei- nigt
Un- cloud- ed now, the
rei- nig' un- sern Glau- ben!
Faith from er- ror sev- er!
rei- nig' un- sern Glau- ben!
Faith from er- ror sev- er!
rei- nig' un- sern Glau- ben!
Faith from er- ror sev- er!
rei- nig' un- sern Glau- ben!
Faith from er- ror sev- er!
p
dim.
dim.
dim.
dim.

523
Cl. 1, 2 in C
Bn. 1, 2
Druide [2]
sich vom Rauch: so rei- nig' un- sern Glau- ben! Und
flame is bright! Thus Faith from er- ror sev- er! Though
Vn. 1
Vn. 2
p
Va.
divisi
p
[unisono]
Vc.
Cb.
526
Cl. 1, 2 in C
Tpt. 1, 2 in C
soli
p
Timp.
p
tr
Druide [2]
raubt man uns den al- ten Brauch: Dein Licht,
Foes may cloud or quell our light; Yet Thine,
Vn. 1
p
Vn. 2
Va.
Vc.
Cb.

529
cresc.
mf
dein Licht, wer kann es rau-
Yet Thine, shall shine for ev-
(tr)

*See Text-Genetic Remarks (II: mm. 535–54) and Appendix II.10.

536
f
f
tr
Rauch: So rei- nig' un- sern Glau- ben! Und raubt man
bright! Thus Faith from er- ror sev- er! Though Foes may
Rauch: So rei- nig' un- sern Glau- ben! Und raubt _ man
bright! Thus Faith from er- ror sev- er! Though Foes _ may
Rauch: So rei- nig' un- sern Glau- ben! Und raubt man
bright! Thus Faith from er- ror sev- er! Though Foes may
Rauch: So rei- nig' un- sern Glau- ben! Und raubt man
bright! Thus Faith from er- ror sev- er! Though Foes may

539
Fl. 1, 2
Ob. 1, 2
Cl. 1, 2 in C
Bn. 1, 2
Hn. 1, 2 in C
Tpt. 1, 2 in C
Trb. 1, 2
Trb. 3
CHOR DER DRUIDEN [UND DES HEIDENVOLKS]
S
A
T
B
sf
uns den al- ten Brauch: Dein Licht, wer kann es
cloud or quell our light; Yet Thine, shall shine for
Vn. 1
Vn. 2
Va.
Vc.
Cb.

542
a 2
a 2
rau- ben! Und __ raubt man uns den al- ten Brauch, und __
ev- er! Though Foes may cloud or quell our light; Though
rau- ben! Und __ raubt man uns den al- ten Brauch, und __
ev- er! Though Foes may cloud or quell our light; Though
rau- ben! Und __ raubt man uns den al- ten Brauch, und __
ev- er! Though Foes may cloud or quell our light; Though
rau- ben! Und __ raubt man uns den al- ten Brauch, und __
ev- er! Though Foes may cloud or quell our light; Though

545
Fl. 1, 2
Ob. 1, 2
Cl. 1, 2 in C
Bn. 1, 2
Hn. 1, 2 in C
Tpt. 1, 2 in C
Trb. 1, 2
Trb. 3
CHOR DER DRUIDEN [UND DES HEIDENVOLKS]
S
A
T
B
raubt man uns den al- ten Brauch: dein Licht, wer will es
Foes may cloud or quell our light; Yet Thine, shall shine for
Vn. 1
Vn. 2
Va.
Vc.
Cb.

549
a 2
cresc.
cresc.
a 2
f
rau- ben! Und raubt man uns den al- ten Brauch, und
ev- er! Though Foes may cloud or quell our light; Though
rau- ben! Und raubt man uns den al- ten Brauch, und
ev- er! Though Foes may cloud or quell our light; Though
rau- ben! Und raubt man uns den al- ten Brauch, und
ev- er! Though Foes may cloud or quell our light; Though
rau- ben! Und raubt man uns den al- ten Brauch, und
ev- er! Though Foes may cloud or quell our light; Though
f
f
f
f
f

552
Fl. 1, 2
Ob. 1, 2
Cl. 1, 2 in C
Bn. 1, 2
Hn. 1, 2 in C
Tpt. 1, 2 in C
Trb. 1, 2
Trb. 3
Timp.
CHOR DER DRUIDEN [UND DES HEIDENVOLKS]
S
A
T
B
raubt man uns den Brauch: Dein Licht, dein
Foes may cloud our light; Yet Thine, Thy
Vn. 1
Vn. 2
Va.
Vc.
Cb.
cresc.
f
sf
ff
tr

555
ff
tr
Licht, wer kann, dein
light shall shine, Thy

558
Fl. 1, 2
Ob. 1, 2
Cl. 1, 2 in C
Bn. 1, 2
Hn. 1, 2 in C
Tpt. 1, 2 in C
Trb. 1, 2
Trb. 3
Timp.
CHOR DER DRUIDEN [UND DES HEIDENVOLKS]
S
A
T
B
Licht, wer kann es rau- ben!
light shall shine for ev- er!
Vn. 1
Vn. 2
Va.
Vc.
Cb.
mf
tr

561
tr
cresc.
[cresc.]
f
Wer kann es rau- ben!
shall shine for ev- er!
cresc.

564
Fl. 1, 2
Ob. 1, 2
Cl. 1, 2 in C
Bn. 1, 2
Hn. 1, 2 in C
Tpt. 1, 2 in C
Trb. 1, 2
Trb. 3
Timp.
CHOR DER DRUIDEN [UND DES HEIDENVOLKS]
S
Wer kann es rau- ben, kann es rau-
Thy light, Thy light shall shine for ev-
A
Wer kann es rau- ben, kann es rau-
Thy light, Thy light shall shine for ev-
T
wer kann, wer kann es rau-
Thy light shall shine for ev-
B
wer kann, wer kann es rau-
Thy light shall shine for ev-
Vn. 1
Vn. 2
Va.
Vc.
Cb.

*See Text-Genetic Remarks (II: mm. 568–69) and Appendix II.11.

Appendix I

Passages from No. 1 Excised or Revised after ca. July 1831

Appendix I.1

48
48A
48B
Fl. 1, 2
Ob. 1, 2
Cl. 1, 2
in C
Bn. 1, 2
Hn. 1, 2
in C
Tpt. 1, 2
in D
Trb. 1, 2
Trb. 3
Timp.
tr
Vn. 1
Vn. 2
Va.
Vc.
Cb.

48C
48D
49
f
tr
f

Appendix I.2

64
64A
64B
64C
Fl. 1, 2
Ob. 1, 2
Cl. 1, 2
in C
a 2
Bn. 1, 2
Hn. 1, 2
in C
Tpt. 1, 2
in D
Trb. 1, 2
Trb. 3
Timp.
Vn. 1
Vn. 2
Va.
Vc.
Cb.

64D
64E
64F
65
a 2
f
a 2
f
a 2
f
f

Appendix I.3

[ritardando]
82
82A
82B
82C
82D
Fl. 1, 2
Ob. 1, 2
Cl. 1, 2
in C
Bn. 1, 2
Hn. 1, 2
in C
Trb. 1, 2
Trb. 3
Timp.
[ritardando]
Vn. 1
Vn. 2
Va.
Vc.
Cb.

Tempo
82E
82F
82G
82H
83
1
p
p dolce
tr
pp
Tempo

Appendix I.4

201
201A
201B
201C
a 2
Fl. 1, 2
Ob. 1, 2
Cl. 1, 2
in C
Bn. 1, 2
Hn. 1, 2
in C
Tpt. 1, 2
in D
Trb. 1, 2
Trb. 3
Timp.
Vn. 1
Vn. 2
Va.
Vc.
Cb.
f
cresc.
tr

201D
201E
202
203
ff
sf
dim.
f

Appendix I.5

225
225A
225B
225C
225D
Fl. 1, 2
Ob. 1, 2
Cl. 1, 2 in C
Bn. 1, 2
Hn. 1, 2 in C
Tpt. 1, 2 in D
Trb. 1, 2
Trb. 3
Timp.
Vn. 1
Vn. 2
Va.
Vc.
Cb.
[cresc.]
al
[al]
cresc. al
cresc.

225E
225F
229
230
ff
ff
ff
ff
ff
ff
ff
tr
f
f
f
f
f
f

Appendix I.6

247
247A
247B
247C
Fl. 1, 2
Ob. 1, 2
Cl. 1, 2
in C
Bn. 1, 2
Hn. 1, 2
in C
Tpt. 1, 2
in D
a 2
Trb. 1, 2
Trb. 3
Timp.
tr
Vn. 1
Vn. 2
Va.
Vc.
Cb.

247D
248
tr

Appendix I.7

507
507A
507B
507C
Fl. 1, 2
Ob. 1, 2
Cl. 1, 2 in A
Bn. 1, 2
Hn. 1, 2 in D
Druide [1]
Vn. 1
Vn. 2
Va.
Vc.
Cb.
p
espress.
durch den Rauch! So wird das Herz er-
flame shall rise; thus blend our hearts to-

507D
507E
507F
507G
507H
a 2
f
-ho- ben. Be- geht den
-geth- er. Be- gin the

507I
507J
507K
507L
Fl. 1, 2
a 2
f
Ob. 1, 2
a 2
f
Cl. 1, 2 in A
Bn. 1, 2
a 2
f
Hn. 1, 2 in D
Druide [1]
Brauch!
rite!
Die
In
Flam-
sac-
me
ri-
Vn. 1
Vn. 2
Va.
Vc.
Cb.

508
509
510
511
p
cresc.
p
cresc.
p
con fuoco
lod- - re durch den Rauch! So wird das
-fice the flame shall rise! Thus blend our
p
p
cresc.
p
cresc.
p
cresc.
p
cresc.

Appendix I.8

689
689A
689B
689C
689D
690
Fl. 1, 2
Ob. 1, 2
Cl. 1, 2
in A
Bn. 1, 2
Hn. 1, 2
in E
Tpt. 1, 2
in E
Druide [1]
Bran- de! Der Wald ist frei! Das Holz her- bei,
-geth- er! The woods are free! Dis- branch the tree,
Vn. 1
Vn. 2
Va.
Vc.
Cb.

Appendix I.9

701
702
702A
702B
703
a 2
p
a 2
p
pp
p
-len,
-ed;
im
in
Stil-
si-
len,
lence...
und
our
pp
pp
pizz.
pizz.

Appendix I.10

723D
723E
723F
723G
f
sf
Mut
uns
un-
sre
Pflicht
er-
fül-
fear;
show
du-
ty's
claim
re-
spect-
cresc.
[cresc.]
f

724
725
726
Fl. 1, 2
Ob. 1, 2
Cl. 1, 2 in A
Bn. 1, 2
Hn. 1, 2 in E
Tpt. 1, 2 in E
Druide [1]
Vn. 1
Vn. 2
Va.
Vc.
Cb.
a 2
-len. Dann a- ber lasst
-ed! Con- quer with cour- age

Appendix II

Passages from No. 2
Excised or Revised after ca. July 1831

Appendix II.1

Recit[ativo]
Hn. 1, 2 in E
Druide [1]
Die- se dump-fen Pfaf-fen-chris-ten, lasst uns keck sie ü-ber-lis-ten! Mit dem Teu-fel, den sie fa-beln, wol-len wir sie selbst er-
Should our Chris-tian foes as- sail us, aid a scheme that may a-vail us! Feign-ing De-mons whom they fa-ble, We will scare the bi- got
Vn. 1
Vn. 2
Va.
Vc.
Cb.
pp
A Tempo. Andante con moto
-schre-cken. Mit dem Teu- fel, den sie fa- beln, wol- - len wir sie selbst er- schre-cken.
rab- ble. Feign-ing De- mons whom they fa- ble, We will scare the bi- got rab- ble.

Appendix II.2

Appendix II.3

149D
150
151
152
153
a 2
Eu- le, heul' in un- ser Rund- ge- heu- le!
ra- vens, Howl with us and scare the Cra- vens!
Eu- le, heul' in un- ser Rund- ge- heu- le!
ra- vens, Howl with us and scare the Cra vens!

Appendix II.4

*If mm. 283a–d are included, use cue-sized notes in m. 283A.

283C
283D
283E
283F
283G
283H
f
f
divisi
divisi

283I
283J
283K
283L
283M
283N
a 2
Fl. 1, 2
dim.
Ob. 1, 2
dim.
Cl. 1, 2 in C
dim.
Bn. 1, 2
a 2
marcato
Hn. 1, 2 in D
dim.
Tpt. 1, 2 in C
Timp.
[CHOR DES HEIDENVOLKS]
S
A
T
Kommt mit Za- cken, kommt mit Ga- beln,
Come with flap- pers, Fire and clap- pers,
B
Kommt mit Za- cken, kommt mit Ga- beln,
Come with flap- pers, Fire and clap- pers,
Vn. 1
Vn. 2
Va.
Vc.
Cb.

283O
283P
283Q
283R
283S
283T
Kommt! Kommt! Kommt! Kommt!
Come! Come! Come! Come!
Kommt! Kommt! Kommt! Kommt!
Come! Come! Come! Come!
Kommt mit Glut und
Come with hop- sticks,
Kommt mit Glut und
Come with hop- sticks,
pizz.
pizz.

283U
283V
283W
283X
283Y
283Z
Fl. 1, 2
Ob. 1, 2
Cl. 1, 2 in C
Bn. 1, 2
Hn. 1, 2 in D
Tpt. 1, 2 in C
Timp.
[CHOR DES HEIDENVOLKS]
S
Kommt! Kommt! Kommt! Kommt!
Come! Come! Come! Come!
A
Kommt! Kommt! Kommt! Kommt!
Come! Come! Come! Come!
T
Klap- per- stö- cken
Brooms and mop- sticks;
B
Klap- per- stö- cken
Brooms and mop- sticks;
Vn. 1
Vn. 2
Va.
Vc.
Cb.

early deletion
283AA
283x
283y
283z
284
Kommt mit
Come with
Kommt mit
Come with
lär- men wir bei nächt'- ger Wei- le. Heul'!
Thro' the night- gloom lead and fol- low. Howl!
lär- men wir bei nächt'- ger Wei- le. Heul'!
Thro' the night- gloom lead and fol- low. Howl!
arco

Appendix II.5

317G 317H 317I 317J 317K 317L 317M 317N
ff
pp sempre
[in B♭-C]
tr
heul'!
Howl
p
und Eu-
and ra-
-le
-vens

P
317O
317P
317Q
317R
a 2
322
323
Fl. 1, 2
Ob. 1, 2
Cl. 1, 2 in C
Bn. 1, 2
Hn. 1, 2 in D
Tpt. 1, 2 in C
Timp.
in C-G
[CHOR DES HEIDENVOLKS]
S
Kommt mit Za- cken
Come with flap- pers
A
- - le! Kommt mit Za- cken
- - vens Come with flap- pers
T
Kommt!
Come!
B
Kommt!
Come!
Vn. 1
Vn. 2
Va.
Vc.
Cb.

Appendix II.6

Appendix II.7

397
397A
397B
a 2
a 2

397C
397D
398
Fl. 1, 2
Ob. 1, 2
Cl. 1, 2 in C
Bn. 1, 2
Hn. 1, 2 in D
in C
Tpt. 1, 2 in C
Timp.
tr
sfz
mf
dim.
Vn. 1
Vn. 2
Va.
Vc.
Cb.

Appendix II.8

Vivace e con moto
450F
450G
450H
Fl. 1, 2
Ob. 1, 2
Cl. 1, 2 in C
Bn. 1, 2
Hn. 1, 2 in C
Tpt. 1, 2 in C
Trb. 1, 2
Trb. 3
f
[Vivace e con moto]
[Christl.] Wächter
Druide [2]
ben!
er!
[Vivace e con moto]
Vn. 1
pp e stacc.
sempre pp e stacc.
Vn. 2
stacc.
pp
[sempre pp e stacc.]
Va.
stacc.
pp
sempre pp e stacc.
Vc.
Cb.

450I
450J
450K
Hilf, ach hilf mir, Kriegs-ge-sel- le! Ach, es kommt die gan- ze Höl-le!
Help, my Com-rades, see a Le-gion, Yon-der comes from Sa-tan's re-gion!

Appendix II.9

513
514
514A
fsf
p
dim.
flieh'n! Lasst uns flieh'n! Lasst uns, lasst uns al- le flieh'n! Lasst uns flieh'n,
fly! Let us fly! Let us, let us quick- ly fly! Let us fly,
flieh'n! Lasst uns, lasst uns al- le flieh'n! Lasst uns
fly! Let us, let us quick- ly fly! Let us
flieh'n! Lasst uns flieh'n! Lasst uns, lasst uns al- le flieh'n! Lasst uns
fly! Let us fly! Let us, let us quick- ly fly! Let us
515
516
pp
flieh'n! Lasst uns flieh'n!
fly! Let us fly!
flieh'n! Lasst uns flieh'n!
fly! Let us fly!
flieh'n! Lasst uns flieh'n!
fly! Let us fly!
flieh'n! Lasst uns
fly! Let us

Appendix II.10

535C
535D
535E
sf
sf
sf
sf
sf
-ben! Und raubt man uns den al- ten Brauch: Dein
-er! Though Foes may cloud or quell our light; Thy
-ben! Und raubt man uns den al- ten Brauch: Dein
-er! Though Foes may cloud or quell our light; Thy
-ben! Und raubt man uns den al- ten Brauch: Dein
-er! Though Foes may cloud or quell our light; Thy
-ben! Und raubt man uns den al- ten Brauch: Dein
-er! Though Foes may cloud or quell our light; Thy

535F
535G
554
Fl. 1, 2
Ob. 1, 2
Cl. 1, 2 in C
Bn. 1, 2
Hn. 1, 2 in C
Tpt. 1, 2 in C
Trb. 1, 2
Trb. 3
Timp.
CHOR DER DRUIDEN [UND DES HEIDENVOLKS]
S
Licht, wer kann es rau- ben! Dein Licht, dein
light shall shine for ev- er! Yet Thine, Thy
A
Licht, wer kann es rau- ben! Dein Licht, dein
light shall shine for ev- er! Yet Thine, Thy
T
Licht, wer kann es rau- ben! Dein Licht, dein
light shall shine for ev- er! Yet Thine, Thy
B
Licht, wer kann es rau- ben! Dein Licht, dein
light shall shine for ev- er! Yet Thine, Thy
Vn. 1
Vn. 2
Va.
Vc.
Cb.

Appendix II.11

Appendix III

Mendelssohn's Piano-Duet Arrangement of the Overture

Allegro con fuoco
Primo
Secondo
f
sf

18
[cresc.]
[cresc.]
22
f
f
26
30
ff
ff
8va

34
(8va)
38
sf
sf
42
46
f
f

50
54
ff
ff
58
sf
sf
sf
sf
sf
62
sf
sf
sf
sf
8va

(8va)
66
(8va)
70
sf
p
sf
75
sf
sf
80
ritardando
sf
p
p
sf
p
p
[cresc. al]

85
cresc.
sf
f
f
89
cresc.
ff
ff
ff
93
dim.
97
p
p
p

101
105
p
sf
109
113
cresc.
cresc.

117
sempre cresc.
[sempre cresc.]
121
cresc. al
125
ff
ff
129

133
138
f
f
143
148
f

153
158
sf
sf
163
sf
sf
sf
f
sf
168
sf
sf
sf

173
più f
178
8va
ff
ff
(8va)
183
p
p
187
sf
sf
p
sf
sf

191
sf
sf
195
sf
p
sf
199
cresc.
ff
ff
203
sf
dim.
p
dim.
sf
[dim.]
[dim.]

208
pp
[dim.]
pp
213
pp
Ped.
218
stacc.
cresc.
stacc.
cresc.
223
f
più f
f
più f

228
ff
ff
232
sf
236
sf
sf
240
sf

244
248
f
dim.
f
mf
[dim.]
252
p
dim.
sf
p
p
sf
256
sf
p
cresc.
sf
cresc.

260
sf
sf
sf
sf
sf
264
8va
sf
ff
ff
268
(8va)
ff
ff
272
(8va)

276
281
f
ff
f
286
ff
290

294
298
ff
ff
f
dim.
303
p
p
dim.
310

317
pp
pp
Ped.
[※]
324
[cresc.]
p
330
Ped.
[※]
336
Allegro di molto
f

Critical Report

Sources

As is usually the case with Mendelssohn's works, the source-situation of *Die erste Walpurgisnacht* is quite complex. Many sources survive, others are lost, and others are in private possession. In each category, some sources are complete and some are fragmentary. Some appear to be chronologically discrete, while others demonstrably contain two or more layers of revision and alteration. Due to limitations of space, this report discusses in detail only the major sources for the cantata, with emphasis on those directly relevant to this edition. Other sources are described only briefly; sources not relevant to the 1832–33 version are omitted from these remarks.[1]

The sigla of lost sources are enclosed in brackets ([ ]). An initial asterisk (*) indicates that the source is fragmentary; i.e., that it appears to have been removed from a more complete manuscript and to lack preceding musical material. Such sources are numbered with reference to the complete source to which they evidently pertain (for example, *[*AS1a]* denotes a fragment that evidently belonged with *AS1* at some point). In the first alphabetic position of source sigla, *Sk* denotes a sketch or draft; *A* denotes an autograph entirely or partially in Mendelssohn's handwriting; sources whose musical text is in another hand, but that also contain entries in Mendelssohn's hand, are designated *A/C*; and *E* denotes a printed edition. In the second capitalized position *S* denotes "score," while *P* denotes "part." Thus, *AS* refers to an autograph score while *AP* refers to an autograph vocal or instrumental part. *Pf* refers to a score (= part) for piano solo or piano duet.

Primary Source

AS1

Kraków, Biblioteka Jagiellońska, Mus. ms. autogr. F. Mendelssohn Bartholdy 37. Autograph full score with additional markings in other hands; sixty-six oblong leaves, in green binding (probably by Mendelssohn[2]) and within a librarian's case. The leaves evidently were originally arranged as a regular series of bifolia, but the structure is now irregular in places due to the removal of individual leaves and the insertion of various paste-overs. One page or bifolio has been separated from the volume entirely and is now lost, as have two paste-overs.[3] Headed simply "Die erste Walpurgisnacht," the first page of *AS1* includes the invocation "H.D.[m.]"[4] ("Hilf Du mir," equivalent to "Help Thou me") in its upper right-hand corner. Beginning around 1832, Mendelssohn typically inscribed this prayer at the head of his manuscripts whenever he entered a new and/or significant phase of work. The final page of the score includes two dates of completion in two different inks: "Mailand d[en] 15ten July | 1831" and "Paris den 13ten Februar | 1832."

Autograph page numbers in *AS1* originally ran from 1 (the first page of score) to 123, but this sequence was disturbed by the subsequent removal of pages. There is also a set of page numbers in the handwriting of Albert Kopfermann, former head of the music division of the Königliche Bibliothek zu Berlin (now the Staatsbibliothek zu Berlin–Preußischer Kulturbesitz), to which a sizeable portion of Mendelssohn's musical estate was donated by his heirs in 1878.[5] These remarks and the critical notes will cite both page numbers when they are applicable, with Mendelssohn's and Kopfermann's paginations separated by a slash (e.g., "p. 49/53").

Beneath the systems in the pages for the vocal portions of *AS1* there is also a series of penciled markings, evidently autograph. These markings begin on page 47/51 beneath I: measure 513 and alternate between arabic numerals and "x" approximately every 4 to 6 measures. Since these numbers occur less frequently during the passages for vocal soloists,[6] it seems probable that they were copied into the instrumental and/or choral parts used for the private performance in Berlin in November 1832 and/or the public premiere in January 1833, serving as rehearsal letters for the ensemble performers. For our purposes, they are also useful indicators of material that had been deleted prior to the first documented performance with chorus, which took place in the Mendelssohn family home in Berlin on 11 October 1832 (see introduction, p. xv).

AS1 clearly served as Mendelssohn's composition score for some period of time. Its many layers of revision are reflected not only by the interrupted page sequence and various revised, cross-hatched, or otherwise deleted passages, but also by autograph entries written with several different writing utensils. The main *Notentext* is written in brown ink, but a number of revisions and some entire pages are written in black ink. Since the final date entered in Milan (15 July 1831) is in brown ink and the date entered in Paris is in black ink, we may conjecture that at least some of the revisions in black ink were entered during Mendelssohn's Parisian sojourn (9 December 1831–19 April 1832).[7] Additional autograph notations in pencil were evidently entered at a very late date—perhaps when Mendelssohn was using *AS1* as the starting point for writing out the second complete orchestral score (see under *AS2*, below). There are also entries in the handwriting of Mendelssohn's older sister, Fanny Hensel; these are indicated in the critical notes, below.

Other Sources Relating to the 1832–33 Version

Sk1

Oxford, Bodleian Library, Mus. M. Deneke Mendelssohn c. 47, fol. 29r. Sketch, 4 measures, for strophe 6 (mid-October 1830).[8]

Sk2

Staatsbibliothek zu Berlin–Preußischer Kulturbesitz, Mus. ms. autogr. F. Mendelssohn Bartholdy 18, p. 39–42. Sketches for the overture and an incomplete page of score for nine measures of strophe 6 ("Verteilt euch wackre Männer hier"). The page of score was written and removed from *AS1* before 15 July 1831. The sketches for the overture almost certainly date from between then and January 1832.[9]

[*AS1a]

Autograph beginning of the overture with slow beginning (Andante) in G minor, $\frac{3}{4}$, 138 measures; (between 15 July 1831 and 13 February 1832). Auctioned by Hans Schneider (Tutzing, Germany) in 1979; now presumably in private possession.[10]

[*AS1b]

Residue of the glue from the underside of this lost manuscript is present on p. 97 of *AS1.* It was almost certainly autograph and must have transmitted material pertaining to strophe 8, but otherwise nothing is known of its content or structure.

*AS1c

Paris, Bibliothèque nationale de France (Bibliothèque du Conservatoire), Ms. 207. One single sheet in full score transmitting an early version of the close of strophe 10 and beginning of strophe 11. This autograph fragment is the source for this edition's text of II: measures 451–68. In 1979 and 1982 Douglass Seaton, writing before *AS1* had resurfaced, conjectured that **AS1c* dated from before 14 July 1831; in 1997, however, Christoph Hellmundt, comparing it with the recently recovered *AS1* and the 1842–44 autograph score *(AS2),* found evidence suggesting a later date.[11] Nevertheless, the paper, ink, and writing utensil of **AS1c* are identical to those of the main *Notentext* of *AS1,* clearly indicating that it was a part of that autograph's compositional history. Moreover, the first measure of **AS1c* follows directly from the penciled corrections to the last undeleted measure of *AS1* p. 112, and the last notated measure of fol. 2v of **AS1c* leads directly into the first measure of *AS1* p. 114, the recto side of which (p. 113) retains signs of a now-deleted paste-over. These notational linkages confirm that **AS1c* was at some point either a part of *AS1* or intended to be so. Hellmundt's suggestion that **AS1c* dates from later than 13 February 1832 is probably correct, but the argument that it may date from as late as 1842 is untenable.

[*AS1d]

Residue of the glue from the underside of this lost manuscript is present on p. 113 of *AS1.* The manuscript was almost certainly autograph and must have transmitted material pertaining to strophe 10 (and perhaps also the end of strophe 9), but otherwise nothing is known of its content or structure.

APf1

Staatsbibliothek zu Berlin–Preußischer Kulturbesitz, 2 an: Mus. ms. autogr. F. Mendelssohn Bartholdy 49. Holograph arrangement for piano-duet four hands, corresponding to "bad weather" and "transition to spring" of *AS1.* An edition of this autograph is included in this volume as Appendix III. It clearly served as a composition score, since the primo and secondo parts are written in score form rather than on facing pages (as was usual). The primo (treble) part is fully notated except for some slurs, dynamics, and other expressive indications, while the secondo part is only partially notated.[12]

AP1

New Haven, Connecticut, Yale University Music Library, SC Ma21 / M522 / Er87. Autograph tenor part,[13] with no title or other heading and many deletions and corrections. This manuscript transmits an early version of the tenor part, beginning at Part I, measure 399, and extending through the original version of the introduction to no. 2 (II: m. 25). As noted under *AS1,* earlier, this version of the opening of no. 2 was at some point replaced by a paste-over transmitting the version given in this edition.

[AP2]

Autograph tenor part headed "Ein Druide." Fair copy with no corrections or changes, corresponding to the "Druide" part for the early version as given in *AS1.*[14]

[A/CP]

Parts for other soloists, chorus, and orchestra used for the performances in Berlin (11 November 1832 and/or 10 January 1833). Some or all of these parts may have been autograph (as *AP1* and *AP2* are) or contained autograph corrections and changes.

Sources Relating to the 1843–44 Version[15]

AS2

Leipzig, Musikbibliothek der Stadt Leipzig, shelfmark PM 143. Autograph full score of the final version (op. 60), fair copy with corrections introduced in three major stages of revision.[16] The volume presumably was bound at

Mendelssohn's direction, as it is included in his *Musikalien* inventory of November 1844.[17] It also includes an appended score for piccolo, three trombones, bass drum, and cymbals (those instruments' music for the final version of nos. 5–7, corresponding to II: mm. 1–389 of this edition). The final page of the main score is dated "Mailand 1831 (d[en] 15ten July) | Paris 1832 (d[en] 13ten Februar), Leipzig 1842. (im Dezember.) | beendigt Leipzig 1843 (den 15ten July)."

*AS2a

Staatsbibliothek zu Berlin–Preußischer Kulturbesitz, Mus. ms. autogr. F. Mendelssohn Bartholdy 56. Autograph full-score fragment for strophe 8, with the autograph pagination "85–88." The lower margin bears the inscription "Herrn Landsberg zum Andenken an gute alte Zeit und an Felix Mendelssohn Bartholdy. Leipzig d. 4ten Sept. 1843."

APf2

Tokyo, Museum of Educational Heritage (Kyouiku Hakubutsukan) at Tamagawa University. Autograph piano/vocal score based on *AS2*, produced in late spring/early summer of 1843. This newly recovered source, already discussed in detail by Hiromi Hoshino, has been published in full-color facsimile by Yoshodo (Tokyo) in 2006.[18]

EPf1

First edition of piano/vocal score, published by Friedrich Kistner (Leipzig) and Ewer & Co. (London), ca. 1 February 1844 (plate number 1400);[19] also distributed by Benacci & Peschier (Lyons and Paris). The English text was provided by William Bartholomew.[20] The music and German text largely correspond to that in *APf2*, although there are some significant differences. The edition was also consulted in preparing the reconstructed material in this volume's edition of *APf1* (Appendix III).

ES1

First edition of the orchestral score, published by Friedrich Kistner (Leipzig) and Ewer & Co. (London), ca. April 1844 (plate no. 1403.) Based on *AS2*.

Editorial Methods

The main source for the orchestral and vocal parts of present edition is *AS1* (see above), the holograph full score for the early version of *Die erste Walpurgisnacht*. When ambivalent information occurs in this source and another source offers a clearer valid reading at an analogous point, the edition incorporates the clearer reading and explains the decision in the critical notes. Significant deletions and revisions are identified under "Text-Genetic Remarks" in the critical notes and reproduced in the appendices.

As is usually the case in such matters, editorial decisions are suggestions only; they may be altered or disregarded at the performer's discretion. All editorial decisions are differentiated from authorial notations either in the body of the score itself, in the critical notes, or in the following list of guidelines:

1. The score order has been modernized: While Mendelssohn places the timpani between the trumpets and trombones and the vocal parts between the violas and violoncellos, in this edition brass and strings each are grouped together, with timpani and vocal parts between the two. In *AS1*, all three trombones are sometimes notated on one staff, in bass clef; in the edition, trombone 3 has a separate staff throughout. Likewise, violoncellos and contrabasses, mostly sharing a staff labeled "Bassi" in *AS1*, have been separated. Due to space restrictions in *AS1* even the two violin parts share a staff in extended passages; in the edition they have separate staves throughout.
2. Mendelssohn uses soprano (C1) clef for all female vocal parts and tenor (C4) clef for the tenor parts. In this edition, the C clefs in the vocal parts have been replaced by treble clef for soprano and alto and transposing treble clef for tenor. The alto (C3) clef for trombones 1 and 2 has been retained.
3. Rehearsal letters provided in *AS1* extend only through "G" (I: m. 379). The remainder of this edition's rehearsal letters are included by analogy with the published first score edition *(ES1)*.
4. Editorial accidentals are enclosed in brackets ([ ]). Unless subsequently canceled, these accidentals are valid to the end of the affected measure. When writing simultaneous octaves that required sharps or flats within a single staff, Mendelssohn often made do with a single accidental (usually placed before the upper note); this edition marks the extra accidentals as editorial.
5. Editorial cautionary accidentals are enclosed in parentheses. Redundant accidentals present in the autograph are retained as courtesy accidentals.
6. Editorial slurs and ties appear dashed.
7. Editorial dynamic indications are provided in roman font.
8. Variant forms of the words *crescendo* and *diminuendo* ("crescendo," "cres.," "cresc.," "diminuendo," "dimin.," "dim.") are tacitly regularized to *cresc.* and *dim.*
9. Editorially supplied extensions of crescendo or diminuendo directions are indicated through dashed doubled-ended brackets (└-------┘).
10. Editorial expressive markings are enclosed in brackets.
11. Staccato dots, which in the source often appear on the side of the stem, have been moved to the notehead according to modern practice in instrumental parts.
12. "C.A." (col arco) is tacitly realized as "arco."
13. Mendelssohn's usual designation for "divisi" is "a 2"; this is tacitly changed to "divisi" throughout.
14. Common stemming versus opposing stemming: In his notation of paired wind instruments, Mendelssohn is inconsistent. Sometimes he uses common stems, sometimes opposing stems. In this edition, common stems are used as far as possible, with "a 2" for unison passages. When two simultaneous notes in a single staff of the autographs share a stem, any articulations, dynamics, and expressive markings are assumed to apply to both.

Conversely, when two simultaneous notes in a single staff have differentiated stems, such markings are applied only individually, to the voice most obviously affected (on the basis of proximity on the page). Any application to the other note is treated as an editorial intervention.

15. Notational abbreviations for repeated measures, repeated beats, octave doublings and transpositions, and *colla parte* doublings are tacitly realized.

16. Editorial completions of words appear in brackets. Conjectures as to ambiguous underlay are identified in the critical notes. The English underlay, which is conjectural throughout, is set in italics. See also the discussion of the English text under "Reconstructed Material," below.

17. In instances where the English underlay makes a melodic alteration necessary for reasons of diction, the suggested alteration is provided in a smaller font within the same staff.

18. Spellings, capitalizations, and word divisions are tacitly adjusted to conform to modern practice. As a rule, punctuation is preserved as given in the original source.

On the whole, the edition avoids regularization of articulations, slurs, dynamics, etc. by analogy to parallel passages elsewhere in the work.[21] In accordance with recent scholarship concerning the editing of nineteenth-century music, the edition retains several important features of Mendelssohn's notation. Most obviously, his use of diamond-shaped crescendo/diminuendo marks (or hairpins, i.e., <>) is retained in differentiation to modern crescendo/diminuendo indications (see the discussion under "Ensemble Issues" in "Notes on Performance"). In addition, dynamic and expressive markings that would appear "ungrammatical" according to modern convention (such as *f* and *sf* applied to the same note) have been retained. The reason for this retention is that many nineteenth-century composers, including Beethoven, Berlioz, Mendelssohn, and Schumann, differentiated between *sf* and *sfz,* while also using the latter interchangeably with accent marks, elongated accent marks, and diminuendo marks in different sources' presentation of the same music. The evident interchangeability of the latter indications suggests that a central component of the idea of *sfz* was that of a rapid decay after the accent. Conversely, it suggests that *sf*, unlike *sfz*, indicated that the emphasis was to be sustained rather than decaying. Viewed this way, *sf* means not *sforzato,* as modern convention assumes, but *subito forte* (delivered with sudden and sustained strength within the operative dynamic context, regardless and whether that context is *f* or *p*). The dual meaning of *forte* as both "loud" and "strong/forceful" thus transforms apparently ungrammatical markings such as the combination of *f* and *sf* on a single note into clarifying interpretive directions—first, by indicating that the affected note(s) are to remain "strong" within a given dynamic level (not necessarily *forte*); and second, by indicating at least some prolongation of the "suddenly forceful" delivery.

Similarly, the edition retains Mendelssohn's "chained" slur markings rather than regularizing them in accordance with the modern preference for inclusive slurring—essentially the consolidation of all slurs within a single passage under a single slur that extends from the first slurred note to the last unslurred one—because the seeming inconsistency or arbitrariness of his notation is in all probability a deliberate and clarifying guideline for interpretive nuance. Here, too, his use of two or more successive and/or overlapping slurs, sometimes in combination with ties, concurs with that of other early and mid-nineteenth-century composers (Beethoven, Schubert, Berlioz, and Schumann, for example). As Hugh McDonald pointed out already in 1969, for nineteenth-century composers and performers the slur possessed at least five different connotations: (1) a tie; (2) an irregular grouping of notes (such as a triplet); (3) legato; (4) lengths of phrases or note-groupings; and (5) expressive nuance that affects dynamics and duration. The first four of these lend (or adapt) themselves well to assumptions about modern inclusive slurring; the latter resists such consolidation. In addition to their implications concerning bowing and breathing,[22] these slur-elisions can help to draw attention to small expressive units within longer legato phrases (and to solicit performers to draw attention to them accordingly), or, at the point where two or more successive slurs elide or intersect, to indicate the point of expressive weight within longer legato phrases.[23]

Finally, since seemingly lacking ties and seemingly premature terminations of trill-extension signs in the timpani notation may imply a reiteration, the edition reproduces these as given in the source. Similarly, since note-groupings, abbreviations, fingered tremolos, and irregular beamings can suggest subtle departures from normal practice, these are retained in the text when their retention does not depart significantly from accepted modern conventions of notation.[24] Other instances of such groupings and abbreviations are identified as notational variants (section 2 of the critical notes).

Reconstructed Material

Despite its generally complete state, *AS1* is lacking two paste-overs and a single leaf at the end of strophe 9 and beginning of strophe 10 (after II: m. 450 in this edition). Most likely removed sometime after Mendelssohn had undertaken to write out the entire score anew in December 1842, the missing page from the end of strophe 9 may have been given to someone as a memento (as Mendelssohn is known to have done with pages from individual scores after they were no longer of use to him, and as he evidently did with source **AS1c*). The exact contents of this page will remain undetermined unless the removed leaf resurfaces. Fortunately, the Paris score fragment (source **AS1c*) probably offers a valid indication of what the content of the missing leaf from *AS1* may have been—problematical only in its inclusion of female voices in a scene that is otherwise entrusted only to male voices. The female voices foreshadow the 1843–44 version. This edition's reconstruction of the passage therefore is based on **AS1c*. The *post-correcturam* reading of the "loose ends" around the gap in *AS1*—four measures following Part II, measure 450 and seven measures preceding Part II, measure 469—is given in Appendix II.8.

Also qualifying as reconstruction, albeit in a broader sense of the term, is the English text included in this edition. The sources for the 1832–33 version include no English underlay, but as discussed in the introduction, Mendelssohn was fully fluent in English, and he cultivated extensive interactions with England's vibrant musical culture throughout his professional career. He was more than eager to offer most of his vocal music to English-language performers and listeners, and he corresponded extensively and in remarkable detail with William Bartholomew, the translator who provided the English version of Goethe's poem when the final version of the *Walpurgisnacht* was published in 1844.[25] For that reason, this edition also includes Bartholomew's 1844 English text as a viable option for English-language performers who wish to realize the work in that version.

Finally, the piano reduction for measures 1–340 of the overture, included here as Appendix III, follows the autograph piano-vocal arrangement of the version of 1832–33 (see discussion of source *APf1*, above). Because *APf1* provides few incidentals (dynamic and expressive markings, etc.), those missing are applied after the model of the orchestral score and treated as editorial interventions. When the omitted material in the secondo part of *APf1* has a clear counterpart in Mendelssohn's piano-duet arrangement of the 1842–44 version, this reconstruction is modeled after that source and the first edition thereof (see under *APf2* and *EPf1*, above). All such reconstructed music is provided in a smaller font. The English underlay appears in italics.

Critical Notes

Composers and performers alike can readily attest to the deeply intuitive relationship between composition and notation on the one hand and notation and performance on the other. Because of this self-evident but obviously subjective relationship, the idiosyncrasies of manuscript notation naturally convey important information concerning composers' ideas of their music, as well as offering potentially valuable cues for interpreters. Unfortunately, these notational peculiarities run contrary to the spirit of even the most nuanced musical engraving, since the objective authority of the latter rests largely on its success in privileging universalized consistency (within modern notational protocols) over individualized nuance. Some of these nuances (such as, in $\frac{2}{4}$ time, the division of four eighth notes into individually flagged notes rather than grouping them as two pairs of notes or one group of four notes) may be easily accommodated with the norms of modern notational convention; others are more resistant. The difficulties of the latter group are compounded when the text was never translated into printed form by the composer himself, as in the case of the first version of *Die erste Walpurgisnacht*. And, of course, intuition's tendency toward inconsistency diminishes any hopes for objectively verifiable consistency in the notation itself.

In acknowledgment this methodological paradox, and in the hope that this acknowledgment will empower performers and analysts, this edition's critical notes recognize three classes of textual judgment calls. The first of these, best described as text-genetic remarks, identifies and explains significant features of the manuscript sources (principally *AS1* and **AS1c*) that relate to the work's chronology and to editorial decisions of textual authority. The second class, identified here as notational variants, comprises instances where the manuscript notation conveys some information concerning note-groupings, phrasings, or articulations that does not lend itself readily to transcription in modern notational practice. The third class is the variety of editorial judgment-calls always represented in critical notes: instances where the manuscript sources provide seemingly incomplete, obviously incorrect, or self-contradictory information that requires editorial intervention. The notes conclude with remarks on the twenty-two appendices (I.1–10, II.1–11, III).

The following abbreviations are used for instrumentation: Fl. = flute; Ob. = oboe; Cl. = clarinet; Bn. = bassoon; Hn. = horn; Tpt. = trumpet; Trb. = trombone; Timp. = timpani; S = soprano; A = alto; T = tenor; B = bass; Vn. = violin; Va. = viola; Vc. = violoncello; Cb. = contrabass; Str. = strings. Used in the notes to Appendix III only are 1mo = primo; 2ndo = secondo; r.h. = right hand; l.h. = left hand. Pitch names are given as represented in the respective staves rather than transposed to concert pitch; c′ refers to middle C.

1. *Text-Genetic Remarks*

The following inventory identifies deleted readings of one or more measures and specifies the date at which the deletion was made when this can be determined. Sources are identified according the nomenclature specified above. The following notes refer to locations within the *Walpurgisnacht* according to the part ("I" for the *Einleitung* and "II" for no. 2), measure number, and (as applicable) beat(s) within the measure(s). Unless noted otherwise, all comments refer to source *AS1*.

[No. 1:] Einleitung

Mm. 48–49. Four measures between these two are cross-hatched; see Appendix I.1. The deletion presumably occurred before November 1832, since the measures are not included in *APf1*.

Mm. 57–64. These measures were at some point crossed out in pencil; however, their retention in *APf1* (see Appendix III) and the presence of the penciled autograph rehearsal letter "A" above measure 57 suggest that the deletion occurred only very late, after Mendelssohn had parts produced for the public premiere in January 1833. Moreover, since the measures appear to be present in the earliest surviving sketches belonging to the revisions of 1840–44,[26] it is possible that he crossed them out only much later, before he decided that the revisions would be so extensive that the score would have to be written out anew. Since that deletion evidently postdates the performance of January 1833, this passage has been included in the main text of the edition.

Mm. 64–65. Six measures between these two were cross-hatched in two stages; see Appendix I.2. The excision presumably occurred before November 1832, since the measures are not included in *APf1*.

Mm. 82–83. Eight measures between these two are cross-hatched; see Appendix I.3. The deletion presumably occurred before November 1832, since the measures are not included in *APf1*.

M. 183. This measure was at some point crossed out; however, its retention in *APf1* suggests that the deletion occurred only after the private Berlin performance in November 1832 (see Appendix III). It has been retained in the main text of the edition.

Mm. 201–2. Five measures between these two are cross-hatched; see Appendix I.4. The deletion presumably occurred before November 1832, since the measures are not included in *APf1*.

Mm. 228–29. Six measures between these two were replaced with a paste-over containing mm. 226–28. The original reading is given in Appendix I.5.

Mm. 247–48. Four measures between these two are cross-hatched; see Appendix I.6. The deletion presumably occurred before November 1832, since the measures are not included in *APf1*.

Mm. 473–79. This edition gives the second reading of this transition. Page 43/47 of *AS1* also transmits a similar, but cross-hatched, version comprising four measures that continue the crescendo and accelerando, and five measures of "All^{o} con fuoco." Since the last nine measures of this recto side were deleted and replaced by similar music on the verso of the same leaf, we may surmise that the revision was made immediately or very nearly so (before the composer turned the page).

Mm. 507–8. Thirteen measures between these two are cross-hatched; see Appendix I.7. When the deletion was made is unclear.

Mm. 533–34. Six measures after m. 533 are cross-hatched in ink, followed by a page break (pp. 48/52–49/53). The deleted measures do not connect with m. 534. Rather, they generally correspond to mm. 538–43.

Mm. 689–90. Four measures between these two are cross-hatched; see Appendix I.8. When the deletion was made is unclear. Mendelssohn did not adjust the underlay.

Mm. 702–3. Two measures between these two are cross-hatched; see Appendix I.9. When the deletion was made is unclear.

Mm. 723–24. Seven measures between these two are cross-hatched; see Appendix I.10. When the deletion was made is unclear.

Mm. 794–97. *AS1* has three measures only (794–96), cross-hatched in ink; at a later stage, Mendelssohn reinstated the measures with the word "gilt" (is valid) and added the direction "bis" to indicate a repeat of measure 796. With the reinstatement of these measures, the interim underlay of mm. 791–93, "Verteilt euch, wackre Männer, hier," was discarded as well.

No. 2

Mm. 1–10. At some point these measures were cross-hatched. However, the version given here is the second version of the slow introduction to no. 2 and is pasted over the original version. The ink with which the version given here was written matches that with which Mendelssohn inscribed the date of "Paris den 13ten Februar 1832" at the end of the score, thus suggesting that the replacement occurred at that late date. Since it seems improbable that no. 2 would open without any introduction, the deletion of these measures may well have occurred when Mendelssohn began contemplating the post-1833 revisions but before he decided that the score would have to be written out anew. The original version of the slow introduction is given as Appendix II.1.

Mm. 54–55. One measure between these two is cross-hatched; see Appendix II.2. When the deletion was made is unclear.

Mm. 142–49. These measures were at some point cross-hatched, but the deletion appears to have been very late: the presence of the rehearsal cue "37" (see discussion of *AS1,* above) within the passage suggests that it was still intact when the parts for the 1833 premiere were produced; the erratic cross-hatching appears to have been entered in haste; and the writing implement with which the cross-hatching was made appears in no revisions to the actual notes. The same grade of cross-hatching, made with the same writing implement, is found at II: mm. 212–19 and II: mm. 312–17. The passage has been retained.

Mm. 149–50. Four measures between these two are cross-hatched; see Appendix II.3. Precisely when they were deleted is unclear, but the voice-leading and text show that the deletion occurred before the cross-hatching of II: mm. 142–49.

Mm. 212–19. These measures were at some point cross-hatched, but the deletion appears to have been very late: the presence of the rehearsal cues "X" and "46" (see discussion of *AS1,* above) within the passage suggests that it was still intact when the parts for the 1833 premiere were produced. The cross-hatching and writing implement correspond to those of II: mm. 142–49 and II: mm. 312–17. The passage has been retained.

Mm. 283–84. *AS1* transmits a total of thirty-five measures that were originally between these two measures, and these measures were deleted in two stages; see Appendix II.4. In addition, the paste-over that originally covered measures 283H–AA of Appendix II.4 is lost (source *[*AS1b]*). Within *AS1*, mm. 283 AA does not connect with m. 284; if Appendix II.4 is to be included in performance, mm. 283x–z are indispensable. The missing collette and the complexity of the revisions in this passage make it impossible to determine when these measures were eliminated, but the absence of any rehearsal cues suggests that the revision occurred before the parts for the Berlin premiere were copied out.

Mm. 312–13. These two measures are cross-hatched. As suggested by the underlay, they were probably deleted at the same time as II: m. 314–17. The passage has been retained.

Mm. 314–17. These measures were at some point cross-hatched. The cross-hatching and writing implement correspond to those of II: mm. 142–49, II: mm. 212–19, and II: mm. 312–13 indicating that the deletion occurred very late, probably after the parts for the 1833 Berlin premiere had been written out. The passage has been retained.

Mm. 317–18. Sixteen measures between these two are cross-hatched; see Appendix II.5. Precisely when they were deleted is unclear, but the voice-leading and text show that the deletion occurred before the cross-hatching of the remaining measures in II: mm. 312–19.

Mm. 318–19. These measures, written as replacement for the preceding sixteen measures, are cross-hatched. The deletion occurred late and was not included here.

Mm. 320–21. Following the replacement of the sixteen measures given in Appendix II.5 with mm. 318–19, Mendelssohn heavily revised these two measures. The original reading is part of Appendix II.5.

Mm. 352–75. This critical passage—dealing with the *stretto* on the chromatically descending melodic cell (see introduction, pp. xvi–xvii) and the reprise of the main theme of strophe 8—was extensively revised in pencil. Since the rehearsal cues that apparently reflect the parts produced for the Berlin premiere continue uninterrupted in the passage, we may surmise that the passage was still intact at that point. Moreover, since the penciled revisions correspond closely to the version of this passage transmitted in the late autograph score fragment **AS2a,* which originally belonged to **AS2,* they may have been entered as preparatory work for the overhauling of the cantata in the early 1840s. These revisions thus post-date the version of *Die erste Walpurgisnacht* offered by this edition and are not incorporated into it. The specific revisions and deletions are as follows:

> *Mm. 352–58.* These seven measures were at some point cross-hatched in pencil, and numerous other revisions to text and music were introduced in the same pencil.
>
> *Mm. 359–60.* These two measures were left intact, but Mendelssohn penciled in revisions in the vocal parts made necessary by the deletion of the previous seven measures, as well as further revisions in the string parts.
>
> *Mm. 361–62.* Mendelssohn penciled revisions in these parts but ultimately deleted them (also in pencil).
>
> *Mm. 363–64.* Mendelssohn retained these measures but penciled in revisions made necessary by the deletion of the previous two measures.
>
> *Mm. 364–65.* Two measures between these two are cross-hatched in ink; see Appendix II.6.

Example 1.

> *Mm. 369–72.* Mendelssohn at some point cross-hatched these four measures in pencil, evidently in the same pencil and handwriting as II: mm. 352–58.
>
> *Mm. 374–75.* In the same pencil used for the above revisions, Mendelssohn modified the S and A parts so that they quote from the first two measures of the main theme of this strophe.

Mm. 394–95. One measure is cross-hatched in ink between these two; see Appendix II.7.

Mm. 397–98. Four measures are cross-hatched in ink between these two; see Appendix II.7.

Mm. 404–6. These four measures are cross-hatched in the same pencil used for the revisions in II: mm. 352–75. The passage has been retained.

Mm. 420–21. In the same pencil used for the revisions in II: mm. 352–75, Mendelssohn added a measure between these two and changed the B solo note in m. 419 to a half note. The contents of the intervening measure are not specified, except that the B solo line includes a "1." above the staff (indicating a one-measure rest).

Mm. 425–28. In the same pencil used for the revisions in II: mm. 352–75, Mendelssohn revised this passage so that the full chorus sings in octaves (as in mm. 33–36 of no. 7 in the final 1842–44 version).

Mm. 435–38. In the same pencil used for the revisions in II: mm. 352–75, Mendelssohn revised this passage as shown in example 1.

Mm. 450–67. *AS1* transmits four heavily revised measures following II: m. 450 and then breaks off, resuming after an obvious gap in the music with the penultimate measure of strophe 9 as the first measure of page 106/113; the presence of residual glue on that page in turn shows that a paste-over (source *[*AS1d]*) at some point replaced the seven measures given on that page. For a discussion of this edition's solution to this problem, see pp. 320–21. For the measures for this passage transmitted in *AS1*, see Appendix II.8.

Mm. 512–13. Two measures between these two are cross-hatched in ink; see Appendix II.9.

Mm. 514–15. One measure between these two is cross-hatched in ink; see Appendix II.9.

Mm. 536–54. In *AS1,* these measures are transmitted on the first three sides of a single bifolio (pp. 118/125–120/127) that was pasted over the original reading (p. 129). The ink and writing implement with which the revised version was written correspond exactly to those of Mendelssohn's appended date of "Paris den 13ten Februar 1832," so that the revision may be securely dated at ca. mid-February 1832. For the original reading of this passage, see Appendix II.10.

Mm. 568–69. Two measures are cross-hatched in ink between these two; see Appendix II.11.

2. *Notational Variants*

This report identifies instances of two varieties of notational variants: note-groupings that may carry implications for phrasing and/or emphasis, and "fingered tremolos." At issue in both varieties (for performers at least) is the matter of relative stress within the respective note-groups. A group of twelve sixteenth notes on a repeated pitch might suggest a variety of subtle subdivisions of the measure if notated as but these subdivisions (such as a grouping into three quarter-notes, with a slight emphasis or change in articulation on the first of each group) are less likely if the group is approached from the perspective of an "abbreviated" notation: . Much the same holds true for the note-grouping sometimes described as the "fingered tremolo" (a measured alternation between two or more notes, e.g.,). This notation suggests different possibilities for performance than do and . The composer's decision to employ the first or third of these may simply reflect haste and convenience—but in all probability it also reflects his thinking on phrasing, harmonic rhythm, or dynamic shape.

The following notes refer to locations within the *Walpurgisnacht* according to the part (I or II), measure number, and (as applicable) beat(s) within the measure(s). Note-groupings are identified first according to variety: "SH" (shorthand) or "FT" (fingered tremolo), then denomination ("8" for eighth notes, "16" for sixteenth notes, etc.), then duration; the pitches are those given in the main body of the edition. Thus, "FT16, half" denotes (fingered tremolo sixteenth notes, half note). When a range of measures is given, the remark is true for each measure within that range in the specified instrument(s). In accordance with the policy stated above, shorthands that conform readily to accepted modern notational convention are not reported separately. Thus, the note-groupings implied by the beams in the modern figures and differ little or not at all from those of Mendelssohn's frequently encountered shorthands and ; because of this equivalence the present edition tacitly replaces the latter with the former. By contrast, because some modern performers might find amplifications of these figures (and) and other shorthands off-putting or obscure, the edition presents their modern counterparts and reports them here as "notational variants." Unless otherwise stated, all notes refer to *AS1*.

[No. 1:] Einleitung

[Overture.] M. 22, Vc., beats 1–2 are FT16, half. M. 24, Vn. 2, beats 2–3 are SH16, half. M. 25, Vn. 2, beats 2–3 are SH16, half. M. 26, Vn. 1 is FT16, dotted half. M. 27, Fl. 1, Vn. 1, beats 1–2 are FT16, half; Vn. 2 is SH16, dotted half. M. 30, Vn. 1, Vn. 2 are FT16, dotted half. M. 31, Vn. 1, beats 1–2 are FT16, half; Vn. 2 is FT16, dotted half. M. 46, Va., beats 1–2 are SH8, half. M. 47, Vn. 2, Va., beats 2–3 are SH8, half. Mm. 57–58, Fl., Ob., Cl., Bn., Vn. 1, Vn. 2, Va., Vc., Cb. are FT16, dotted half. Mm. 61–62, Fl., Ob., Cl., Bn., Vn. 1, Vn. 2, Va., Vc., Cb. are FT16, dotted half. M. 71, Vn. 1, Vn. 2, beats 2–3 are FT16, half. M. 90, Vc., beats 2–3 are FT16, half. M. 92, Vc., Cb. are FT16, dotted half. M. 93, Vc. is FT16, dotted half; Cb., beats 1–2 are FT16, half. Mm. 94–95, Vc., Cb. are FT16, dotted half. M. 96, Vn. 1, beats 2–3 are FT16, half; Vn. 2 is FT16, dotted half. M. 97, Vn. 1, Vn. 2, Va. are FT16, dotted half. M. 202, Vn. 1, Vn. 2, beats 2–3 are SH16, half; Va. is SH16, dotted half. M. 360, Va., beats 3–4 are FT8, half. M. 379, Va. is FT8, half–FT8, half. M. 380, Va., beats 1–2 are FT8, half. Mm. 382–84, Vc. is FT8, half.

Strophe 2. M. 508, Vn. 1, beats 3–4 are FT8, half. Mm. 509–10, Vn. 1 is FT8, half + FT8, half. M. 541, Vc., Cb. are SH8, whole. M. 552, Va. is SH8, whole. Mm. 554–59, Va. is SH8, wholes. M. 561, Vn. 1, Vn. 2, Va. are SH8, whole. Mm. 563–64, Vn. 2 is SH8, wholes. Mm. 573–74, Vn. 1, Vn. 2, Va. are SH8, wholes. M. 575, Vn. 2 is SH8, whole.

No. 2

Strophe 7. Mm. 59, Hn. is SH8, whole. M. 67, Va. is SH16, half + SH16, half.

Strophe 8. Mm. 99–103, Ob., Cl. are SH8, dotted half. Mm. 108–10, Ob., Bn. are SH8, dotted half. M. 110, Hn. is SH8, dotted half. M. 111, Va. is SH16, dotted half. Mm. 113–15, Tpt. is SH8, dotted half. M. 135, Hn., Tpt. are SH8, dotted half. M. 139 Hn., Tpt., Timp. are SH8, dotted half. Mm. 154–56, Ob. 2, Bn. 2 are SH8, dotted half. M. 159, Hn. 1 is SH8, dotted half. M. 162, Fl. 2, Ob. 2, Hn. 2 are SH8, dotted half. M. 163, Ob. 2, Hn. 2 are SH8, dotted half. M. 164, Fl. 2, Ob. 2, Hn. 2 are SH8, dotted half. M. 167, Hn. 1 is SH8, dotted half. Mm. 174–78, Tpt. is SH8, dotted half. Mm. 182–85, Tpt. 2 is SH8, dotted half. M. 186, Fl. 2, Ob. 2, Hn. 2 are SH8, dotted half. M. 187, Ob. 2, Hn. 2 are SH8, dotted half. M. 188, Ob. 2, Hn. 2 are SH8, dotted half. M. 189, Hn. is SH8, dotted half. M. 191, Hn. 1 is SH8, dotted half. M. 194, Fl. 2, Ob. 2, Hn. are SH8, dotted half. Mm. 195–96, Ob. 2, Hn. are SH8, dotted half. M. 197, Hn. are SH8, dotted half. M. 199, Hn. 1 is SH8, dotted half. Mm. 278–79, Vc., Cb. are SH8, dotted half. M. 282, Vc., Cb. are SH8, dotted half. Mm. 323, 325, 331, 333, Vc., Cb. are SH8, dotted half. Mm. 361–68, Vc., Cb. are FT16, dotted half. M. 386, Hn. is SH8, dotted half. Mm. 400–401, Vn. 1, Vn. 2, Va., Vc. are FT32, half.

Strophe 10. M. 475, Vn. 1, Vc., beats 3–4 are SH16, half. M. 476, Vn. 1, Vn. 2, Va., Vc., beats 3–4 are SH16, half. M. 477, Vn. 1, Vn. 2, Va., Vc., Cb. are SH16, half + SH16, half.

Strophe 11. Mm. 486–88, Vc., Cb. are SH16, half + SH16, half. M. 487, Va., beats 1–2 are SH16, half. M. 489, Vc., Cb., beats 1–2 are SH16, half. M. 501, Va., beats 1–2 are SH16, half. M. 511, Vn. 1, beats 1–2 are FT, half. M. 514, Vn. 1 is SH16, half + SH16, half. Mm. 515–16, Vn. 1 is FT16, half + FT16, half.

3. *Other Textual Variants*

Unless otherwise stated, all notes refer to *AS1*.

[No. 1:] Einleitung

[Overture.] M. 20, Vn. 1, lower notes (a′) not dotted. M. 91, Fl., Ob. 1, 2 use single stem for last 16th note. M. 92, Fl., Ob. 1, 2 use single stem. Mm. 162–63, Fl. 1, 2 use single stem. M. 178, Va., note 1 is a′ only (no e′), emended to match mm. 175–77. Mm. 184–89, Vc., "una corda." M. 203, Vc., Cb., "dim." on beat 3. M. 254, Vc., "una corda." M. 274, Bn., staff empty (neither rest nor content). M. 285, Trb. 1, 2 use single stem for last note. M. 311, Va., note is upstem only; "a 2" (= divisi) appears in m. 312 only. M. 326, double bar is editorial. M. 349, Vn. 2, slur begins on beat 2. M. 376, Bn. 2, tied quarter and 8th note, changed to dotted quarter to match m. 377.

Strophe 1. M. 407, Va., note is half (evident oversight). M. 417, Cl. 2, beats 2–3 are lacking dot on quarter note. M. 475, Str., "sempre accel. e cresc."

Strophe 2. Mm. 479–80, Bn. 1, 2 and Vn. 1 are tied over. This edition deletes the ties because they obviously are retained from the original reading and replicate the corresponding ties in the staves of Cl. and remaining Str., which were deleted (perhaps at the same point when the *sf* was added on the downbeat of m. 480). M. 508, Vn. 2, Va., *p* on beat 2.

Strophe 3. M. 610, Vn. 1, first note was originally a′, slurred and beamed to note 2; notes 3–6 were beamed as a group of four. With the change of note 1, the broken beam became obsolete; it was left standing through an oversight. Mm. 613–14, Vn. 2, originally slurred from m. 613, note 3, to m. 614; second slur later added connecting m. 613, notes 2–3.

Strophe 5. Mm. 666–67, chorus, diamond hairpin begins at the end of m. 665, conflicting with *pp*. M. 690, Druide [1], underlay is editorial; *AS1* has "[her-] bei," which was correct before the cut was made. M. 730, Cl. is erroneously notated as B-flat (concert G-natural). M. 739, beat 1, Str. have reiterated *f* (probably in consequence of page turn). M. 742, Druide [1], triplet bracket and number missing.

Strophe 6. M. 748, Fl. and Cl., parts originally exchanged; Mendelssohn later added "Clarinetti transp." to Fl. staff and "Flauti transpon." to Cl. staff. M. 796, beat 4, chorus has "durch" (oversight created by direction "bis").

No. 2

Strophe 7. M. 1, Timp., the tuning is indicated as "C–G," but Mendelssohn subsequently changed the only Cs in no. 2 to D. Mm. 37–87, Druide [1], part not separately written out; direction "col coro" at m. 36 suggests doubling of T1 as realized in this edition. M. 76, Fl., *p* below note 3.

Example 2.

Strophe 8. M. 115, *AS1* provides no term for the chorus in strophe 8, although the first system during which all four parts occur (p. 80/86; m. 145) is labeled "Der ganze Chor" (the whole chorus). In *ES1* and *EPf1* it is labeled simply "Chor." Mm. 147–53, T, B, both text and music are heavily revised, including some late (evidently post-1833) revisions in pencil; see II: mm. 142–49 and II: mm. 149–50 under "Text-Genetic Remarks," above. Because of these multiple layers of chronologically indeterminate revisions, it is impossible to ascertain precisely which reading was in place for the private and public performances of 1832–33. This edition gives a version that clearly predates the post-1833 alterations but is also revised from the earliest reading. M. 170, Va., "stacc." Mm. 177, beat 2 to m. 178, beat 1, Vc., "stacc." Mm. 193–94, Vn. 1, 2, Va., *pp* between the staves of Vn. 1, 2 (combined) and Vn., close to Va., at m. 193, beat 6. M. 201, Va., beats 1–3, 16th notes written out. M. 202, Va., note 1 is quarter, followed by 8th rest. M. 205, A, note 2 is quarter, followed by 8th rest. Mm. 208–9, Va., illegible; note names *g–d–c–g–e–c–g–d–c–g–c–e* written in Mendelssohn's hand above staff. M. 208, Vc., Cb., note names *d–f–e–d–g–e* written in Mendelssohn's hand below staff. Mm. 210–11, A, temporary deletion reversed by the word "gilt" (is valid) above staff. Mm. 220–22, A, no text; only extender line. M. 283, Hn. 1, 2 are erroneously notated as d′–f′ (concert e′–g′). Mm. 320–21, Tpt. 1, 2, earlier version cross-hatched and illegible; new note names *d* written above and below staff. Mm. 320–21, chorus, this edition gives the corrected ink reading of these two measures, written after the deletion of measures 317A–P in Appendix II.5. At some point Mendelssohn penciled in a choral entry for these two measures, as given in example 2. Since this new entry appears to have been designed only very late—perhaps after the parts for the 1833 premiere were written out (see under "Text-Genetic Remarks," above)—it is not included in

this edition. M. 326, Fl. 1, 2 are notated with only a single stem (may be Fl. 1 only). Mm. 335–39, Bn. 1, 2 are notated with only a single stem, no specification as to whether solo or unison was intended.

Strophe 9. M. 399, Ob., note has *sf*, obviously because it precedes a page break, as a "custos" for the *sf* in m. 400. M. 402 was changed to *p* when II: mm. 404–7 were cross-hatched (see under "Text-Genetic Remarks," earlier). M. 410, Mendelssohn eventually penciled the new dynamic marking of *p* for Hn., Tpt., Trb., and Str., doubtless because a true *forte* entrance would have overpowered the voice of the solo Druid. Since this change was evidently after the parts for the 1833 premiere were written out, this edition retains the original dynamic marking. Mm. 432–33, Bn. 1, slur is broken between m. 432, last note, and m. 433, note 1. Mm. 449–50, Ob., notes are deleted in pencil; deletion seems to be very late. Mm. 454–56, Cb. notated octave lower in **AS1c*.

Strophe 10. M. 460, in **AS1c* the tempo was originally given as "Assai Vivace" above the system, but the "Assai" was subsequently crossed out. Beneath the system the tempo is given as simply "Vivace." In the earlier reading of this passage (*AS1* p. 106/113) the tempo is given as "Vivace e con moto" above the system, "Con moto vivace" in the middle of the system (above the Vn. 1 staff), and "Con moto e vivace" beneath the system. This edition adopts the tempo specification common to all, which also appears to be the final reading in **AS1c:* "Vivace."

Strophe 11. M. 505, Str., *pp e stacc.*

Strophe 12. M. 550, B2, note 1 is dotted; no rest. M. 553, Cl. 2, note 3 (beat 4) is missing.

4. Notes on the Appendices

Appendix I.3

Mm. 82B–82D, Vc., Cb., beats 2–3 are SH8, half.

Appendix I.6

M. 247A, Vn. 2, beats 2–3 are SH16, half. M. 247B, Vn. 2 is SH16, dotted half. M. 247C, Vn. 1 is FT16, dotted half. M. 247D, Vn. 1, beats 1–2 are FT16, half; Vn. 2 is SH16, dotted half.

Appendix I.7

M. 507E, Vn. 1, Vn. 2, beats 3–4 are FT8, half; Va. is FT8, half + FT8, half. M. 507F, Vn. 1, Vn. 2, Va. are FT8, half + FT8, half. M. 507G–H, Vn. 2, Va. are FT8, half + FT8, half. M. 507I, Vn. 1, beats 3–4 are FT8, half; Vn. 2, Va., beats 1–2 are FT8, half. M. 507J, Va. is FT8, half + FT8, half. M. 507K, Vn. 2, Va., beats 3–4 are FT8, half. M. 507L, Vn. 2, Va. are FT8, half + FT8, half.

Appendix I.10

M. 732B, Vc., Cb. beamed as three pairs of 8th notes.

Appendix II.2

Mm. 149A–E, Fl., notes have one stem only without indication which instrument is playing.

Appendix II.4

M. 284, Vn. 1, *pfp;* initial *p* is artifact from revisions to preceding measures.

Appendix II.5

Tuning directions for the timpani have been added. Possibly Mendelssohn rejected this passage because it could not be performed properly with only two timpani available. M. 317P, A, syllable "-le" added editorially; missing from source.

Appendix II.8

M. B, *AS1* gives the tempo in three formulations: above the Fl. staff, as "Vivace e con moto"; above the Vn. 1 staff, as "Con moto vivace"; and beneath the Vc./Cb. staff, as "Con moto e vivace."

Appendix II.11

M. 568A, Timp., note 3 (anacrusis) is 16th in source, preceded by 16th rest; changed to match woodwinds and brass.

Appendix III

M. 41, 1mo, dots lacking on e and g (both hands). Mm. 57–58, 1mo and 2ndo, SH16, dotted half. Mm. 61–62, 1mo and 2ndo, SH16, dotted half. Mm. 66–80, 2ndo, l.h. notated with "8vb" sign. Mm. 95–96, 1mo, change to bass clef occurs before m. 96, note 2. Mm. 96 (from beat 2) to m. 97, 1mo, l.h., SH16, half + SH16, dotted half. Mm. 106–18, beat 2, 1mo, l.h. and 2ndo, r.h. are reversed in source; changed editorially to avoid crossing of hands. Mm. 130–31, 1mo, l.h., SH16, dotted half. M. 137, 2ndo, r.h. notated octave lower; changed to avoid clash with (conjectural) l.h. part. Mm. 179–80, 1mo, SH16, dotted half. Mm. 202–7, 2ndo, r.h. notated in treble clef, with lowest notes crossing staves from m. 204, beat 1, through m. 205, beat 2. M. 248, 2ndo, l.h. materials given in r.h.

Notes

1. For the most complete discussion of the sources to date, see my *Mendelssohn, Goethe, and the Walpurgis Night: The Heathen Muse in European Culture, 1700–1850* (New York: University of Rochester Press, 2007), 107–18. See also Douglass Seaton, "A Study of a Collection of Mendelssohn's Sketches and Other Autograph Material, Deutsche Staatsbibliothek Berlin *Mus. ms. autogr. Mendelssohn 19*" (Ph.D. diss., Columbia University, 1977); R. Larry Todd, "The Instrumental Music of Felix Mendelssohn-Bartholdy: Selected Studies Based on Primary Sources" (Ph.D. diss., Yale University, 1979); Douglass Seaton, "The Romantic Mendelssohn: The Composition of *Die erste Walpurgisnacht*," *Musical Quarterly* 68 (1982): 398–410; Christoph Hellmundt, "Mendelssohns Arbeit an seiner Kantate *Die erste Walpurgisnacht:* Zu einer bisher wenig beachteten Quelle," in *Felix Mendelssohn Bartholdy: Kongreß-Bericht Berlin 1994*, ed. Christian Martin Schmidt (Wiesbaden: Breitkopf & Härtel, 1997), 76–112; Peter Krause, "Mendelssohns dramatische Kantate *Die erste Walpurgisnacht:* Ergänzende Bemerkungen zur Werkgeschichte auf der Grundlage von Untersuchungen des Leipziger Autographs der Letztfassung," in *Musik + Dramaturgie: 15 Studien Fritz Hennenberg zum 65. Geburtstag*, ed. Beate Hiltner-Hennenberg (Frankfurt am Main: Peter Lang, 1997), 101–21; and Hiromi Hoshino, "Ein neu entdecktes Mendelssohn-Autograph in Japan: Der Klavierauszug 'Die erste Walpurgisnacht,' op. 60," *Die Musikforschung* 57 (2004): 151–59.

2. This binding closely resembles that of other volumes that Mendelssohn himself demonstrably had bound. The volume is listed as "Walpurgisnacht (erster Versuch)" (Walpurgisnacht [first attempt]) in Mendelssohn's *Musikalien* inventory of November 1844; see Peter Ward Jones, *Catalogue of the Mendelssohn Papers in the Bodleian Library, Oxford, Vol. III: Printed Music and Books* (Tutzing, Germany: Hans Schneider, 1989), 292. Writing before the Leipzig autograph for the final version had resurfaced, Ward Jones surmised that the inventory's other entry for a *Walpurgisnacht* score was the Leipzig autograph, but this should now be corrected.

3. These pages evidently were removed before the volume passed into the possession of the Berlin Staatsbibliothek, since the librarian's pagination counts both sides of all intact collettes but is not interrupted by the missing page (see under "Text-Genetic Remarks," earlier).

4. At some point the pages of *AS1* were trimmed and some marginal material lost. The "m." of this formula was among these casualties.

5. See my "Knowing Mendelssohn: A Challenge from the Primary Sources," *Notes* 61 (2004): 35–95, esp. 52–56. See also Hans-Günter Klein, *Felix Mendelssohn Bartholdy: Autographe und Abschriften: Katalog*, Kataloge der Musikabteilung, Staatsbibliothek zu Berlin–Preussischer Kulturbesitz: series I: Handschriften, vol. 5 (Munich: G. Henle Verlag, 2003), 7–12.

6. For example, I: mm. 513–85 include the numbers and X's through "9X," but all of the alto solo in strophe 3 (I: mm. 586–636) falls under "10" and "11," while the four-measure alternation begins anew with "12" at strophe 4 (I: m. 637).

7. Some instances of this that seem certain are: bifolio 49/53–52/56 (I: mm. 525–96); single sheet 61/65–62/66 (I: mm. 718–40); single-sheet collette 69/73–[(unnumbered)]/74 (II: mm. 1–25); and single sheet 73/79–74/80 (II: mm. 53–69). Since Mendelssohn's letter of 13 February 1832 states that "a couple of days ago" he had "tidied up the seven [texted] movements a bit" and then written the new date of completion at the end of the score, we may securely assign the original black-ink readings of these pages to ca. 11 February 1832. Conversely, the adjoining material (or, as applicable, the corrections entered in order to effect the replacement of the earlier pages) must date from before then, and the relatively few other changes visible on these pages probably date from afterwards.

8. See R. Larry Todd, "Of Sea Gulls and Counterpoint: The Early Versions of Mendelssohn's *Hebrides* Overture," *Nineteenth-Century Music* 2 (1979): 197–213.

9. See Hellmundt, "Mendelssohns Arbeit," 81.

10. Ibid., 79.

11. Seaton, "The Romantic Mendelssohn," 410; Hellmundt, "Mendelssohns Arbeit," 79.

12. See Seaton, "A Study of a Collection"; further, Klein, *Felix Mendelssohn Bartholdy: Autographe und Abschriften.*

13. Seaton ("The Romantic Mendelssohn," 402 and 410) identified this source as a continuity draft for the 1832–33 version, but Hellmundt has correctly established its correspondence to *AS1* ("Mendelssohns Arbeit," 80).

14. See Hellmundt, "Mendelssohns Arbeit," 80.

15. See ibid., 78–81; and especially chapter 5 of my *Mendelssohn, Goethe, and the Walpurgis Night.*

16. See especially Krause, "Mendelssohns dramatische Kantate"; and chapter 5 of my *Mendelssohn, Goethe, and the Walpurgis Night*, 110–11 and 115–18.

17. See Ward Jones, *Catalogue*, 292.

18. I am deeply grateful to Professor Hoshino for sharing her findings with me in advance of their publication, and for her assistance in gaining access to this source.

19. Mendelssohn wrote to the German publisher (Kistner) acknowledging receipt of his exemplars on 4 February 1844. See Rudolf Elvers, *Felix Mendelssohn Bartholdy: Briefe an deutsche Verleger* (Berlin: Walter de Gruyter, 1968), 326. The important issue of Mendelssohn's dealings with French publishers, particularly Benacci & Peschier, is expertly dealt with in two studies that are at press as of this writing: Cécile Reynaud, "Mendelssohn et ses éditeurs français," and Pietro Zappala, "Mendelssohn and His Italian Publishers," both in *Mendelssohn in the Long Nineteenth Century*, ed. Jacqueline Waeber and Nicole Grimes (Aldershot: Ashgate, forthcoming).

20. I thank Peter Ward Jones for his assistance in gaining access to the exemplar of this source held in the Bodleian Library, Oxford (shelfmark Deneke 102). For a detailed discussion of Bartholomew's text, see my *Mendelssohn, Goethe, and the Walpurgis Night*, 202–10.

21. If performers wish to impose such regularity this may be done easily at their discretion, and without cumbersome editorial annotations and interventions. However, Mendelssohn's surviving correspondence with his publishers reveals that he often rejected such regularization, intervening to request that the engraver reinstate apparent inconsistencies that had been erroneously regularized in previous stages of proof.

22. Clive Brown, "Bowing Styles, Vibrato and Portamento in Nineteenth-Century Violin Playing," *Journal of the Royal Musical Association* 113 (1988): 97–128.

23. For a perceptive discussion of this issue in the context of the music of Berlioz (with whom Mendelssohn's notation shares many idiosyncracies), see Hugh McDonald, "Two Peculiarities of Berlioz's Notation," *Music and Letters* 50 (1969): 25–36, esp. 27–31.

24. See my "From Notation to Edition to Performance: Issues in Interpretation," in *Mendelssohn in Performance*, ed. Siegwart Reichwald (Bloomington: Indiana University Press, forthcoming).

25. See my " 'For you see I am the eternal objector': On Performing Mendelssohn's Music in Translation," in *Mendelssohn in Performance*, esp. 211–21. See also my *Mendelssohn, Goethe, and the Walpurgis Night*, 202–10.

26. Staatsbibliothek zu Berlin–Preußischer Kulturbesitz, Mus. Autogr. F. Mendelssohn Bartholdy 19, p. 71, first system.

Recent Researches in the Music of the Nineteenth and Early Twentieth Centuries
Rufus Hallmark, general editor

Vol.	*Composer: Title*
1–2	Jan Ladislav Dussek: *Selected Piano Works*
3–4	Johann Nepomuk Hummel: *Piano Concerto, Opus 113*
5	*One Hundred Years of Eichendorff Songs*
6	Etienne-Nicolas Méhul: *Symphony No. 1 in G Minor*
7–8	*Embellished Opera Arias*
9	*The Nineteenth-Century Piano Ballade: An Anthology*
10	*Famous Poets, Neglected Composers: Songs to Lyrics by Goethe, Heine, Mörike, and Others*
11	Charles-Marie Widor: *The Symphonies for Organ: Symphonie I*
12	Charles-Marie Widor: *The Symphonies for Organ: Symphonie II*
13	Charles-Marie Widor: *The Symphonies for Organ: Symphonie III*
14	Charles-Marie Widor: *The Symphonies for Organ: Symphonie IV*
15	Charles-Marie Widor: *The Symphonies for Organ: Symphonie V*
16	Charles-Marie Widor: *The Symphonies for Organ: Symphonie VI*
17	Charles-Marie Widor: *The Symphonies for Organ: Symphonie VII*
18	Charles-Marie Widor: *The Symphonies for Organ: Symphonie VIII*
19	Charles-Marie Widor: *The Symphonies for Organ: Symphonie gothique*
20	Charles-Marie Widor: *The Symphonies for Organ: Symphonie romane*
21	Archduke Rudolph of Austria: *Forty Variations on a Theme by Beethoven for Piano; Sonata in F Minor for Violin and Piano*
22	Fanny Hensel: *Songs for Pianoforte, 1836–1837*
23	*Anthology of Goethe Songs*
24	Walter Rabl: *Complete Instrumental Chamber Works*
25	Stefano Pavesi: *Dies irae concertato*
26	Franz Liszt: *St. Stanislaus: Scene 1, Two Polonaises, Scene 4*
27	George Frederick Pinto: *Three Sonatas for Pianoforte with Violin*
28	Felix Mendelssohn: *Concerto for Two Pianos and Orchestra in E Major (1823): Original Version of the First Movement*
29	Johann Nepomuk Hummel: *Mozart's "Haffner" and "Linz" Symphonies*
30–31	Gustav Mahler: *Die drei Pintos: Based on Sketches and Original Music of Carl Maria von Weber*
32	Niels W. Gade: *St. Hans' Evening Play Overture*
33	Charles-Marie Widor: *Symphonie pour orgue et orchestre, opus 42bis*
34	Edvard Grieg: *The Unfinished Chamber Music*
35	Johann Nepomuk Hummel: *Twelve Select Overtures*

36 *Motets for One Voice by Franck, Gounod, and Saint-Saëns*

37 *Topical Song Cycles of the Early Nineteenth Century*

38 Alice Mary Smith: *Symphonies*

39 Franz Lachner: *Two Woodwind Quintets*

40 Elfrida Andrée: *Two Chamber Works*

41 Franz Clement: *Violin Concerto in D Major (1805)*

42 Manuel García: *L'isola disabitata*

43 Samuel Coleridge-Taylor: *Symphonic Variations on an African Air*

44 *Orchestral Lieder (1815–1890)*

45 Alice Mary Smith: *Two Overtures: "The Masque of Pandora" (1878) and "Jason, or The Argonauts and the Sirens" (1879)*

46 Anton Reicha: *Missa pro defunctis (Requiem)*

47 *Quodlibets of the Viennese Theater*

48 Johann Herbeck: *Selected German Works for Unaccompanied Men's Chorus*

49 Felix Mendelssohn Bartholdy: *Die erste Walpurgisnacht: First Complete Version, 1832–33*